BLACK
ROOTEDNESS

54 Poets

FROM AFRICA TO AMERICA

Black Rootedness is a transmigration of words in verse, a Sankofa, 'go back and fetch' work that is a timely anthology Karla Brundage has authorized. Great efforts were made between African and American universities to connect Africans to African-Americans in an exchange rooted in experiences unique to our Black lives. From titles like Nia Wilson, to engaging such poetic works in the plural, Giving Honor to The Gods, The Lies I Swallowed, and How You Say No in Thunder, to name a few, makes this trans-Atlantic word-work worthy of eyes traveling!

— Tureeda Mikell, author of SYNCHRONICITY: The Oracle of Sun Medicine, Co-author/curator of the, Patrice Lumumba Anthology

Black Rootedness conveys vibrant energy with every poem. But more than that, the use of the Japanese poetic Renshi approach creates a positive tension between and across the poets' words, while subtly putting on display their interrelatedness. The editors' prioritization of inclusivity delivers poems of differing style and orientation and challenges the reader to expand our notions of expression, art, and voice. Karla Brundage has once again created a vibrant and deeply compelling poetic work.

— Dr. Christine Sow, Specialist, Global Development Equity, & CEO Humentum

Using an intersectional poetics to create numerous avenues of resonant meaning between two continents literally on opposite ends of the globe, editor Karla Brundage has created a platform for a political conversation that is radically reimagined across the face of globalism. Thus, the 78th Psalmist and Nana Boateng, or Ayodele Nzinga and Koku Kanu don't merely exchange expressions, but build a conversation of meaning into physical manifestation. The 54 writers in this collection expand the borders not just of the world, but the universe of what is possible anywhere in this world.

— Paul Corman-Roberts, author of Bone Moon Palace (Nomadic Press, 2021)

BLACK
ROOTEDNESS

54 Poets

FROM AFRICA TO AMERICA

Edited by Karla Brundage

ELYSSAR  PRESS

Printed in the United States of America

First Printing, 2022
ISBN 979-8-9853686-3-5

Elyssar Press
175 Bellevue Ave
Redlands, CA 92373

www.ElyssarPress.com

Cover Photo by Wanda Sabir
Cover design by Stephanie Aoun Bou Karam
Book design and production by Stephanie Aoun Bou Karam
Editing by Karla Brundage
Contributing editors Allie Rigby and Margaret Pierce
Photography by Iman Gibson

Library of Congress Cataloging-in-Publication Data
Cataloged as: Africana, African American, Poetry, Politics, Travel

Dedication...

This book is dedicated to our African ancestors who crossed the Atlantic in the great maafa, the calamity also known as the Middle Passage. To those who died, to those who are present, and to those who will make the journey home—the sankofa journey—to the motherland. To those who became part of the Americas and to those whose seeds created this grand Diaspora. To those who are with us and those who hold their bitterness cursing from their graves. To the spirits still walking the earth with good will, hoping to redirect those of us who are lost and wounded.

This book is also dedicated to all the artist activists including W. E. B. Du Bois, Malcolm X, Maya Angelou, and Muhammad Ali, who gathered and took a journey home to the great country of Ghana and were welcomed through a Door of Return.

Table of Contents

Part One: East Oakland to East Africa

Part Two: West Oakland to West Africa

About the Exchange...

The sequence of the collection reflects an exchange between partners that features the Renshi poetry style, in which each partner's poem begins with the last line of their partner's response poem, thereby creating a linked conversation. Each partner pair included up to three poems that make up these chapters.

EO >>> EA Poetry Partners

Patrice Lumumba Poetry Collective in East Oakland Meets University of Kenya, Kisii

adrienne and Kelvin
Chase and Alfred
Dajuan and Lewis
Darius and Cornelius
Dee Allen. and Evans
Halima and Caren
LadiRev and Rebeccah
Landon and Josephat
Mimi and Stanley
Seestah IMAHKÜS and Dr. Okemwa
Tessa and Lilian
Tongo and Bonface
Zakiyyah and John

WO >>> WA Poetry Partners
West Oakland Community Meets Cultural Intellectual Association of
Lagos, Nigeria

Amos and Godfrey
ayodele and Koku
Duana and Durotinu
Elaine and Uchechi
Iman and Juliet
Imani and Victory
Iris and Matthew
Kevin and Ifeanyichuku
Lisa and Adeyinka
Makeda and Isinaego Josephmark
Meg and Michael
Nana and David
Shawna and Rhema Sunshine
Wanda and Gemini

Introduction

by Rashidah Ismaili

Putting together an anthology is a daunting effort. Melding voices and issues, forms and styles—these pose hurdles for anthologists. Most such collaborations are by an author-driven selection process that values both the writer and their work in the collection. In the case of *Black Rootedness: 54 Poets from Africa to America*, poets are joined by communal bonds interlocking, as well as by building on previous words and content. The result is unity and a community of writers.

In 2013, Karla Brundage—a driving force for this collection—had the opportunity to live in Côte d'Ivoire, West Africa to teach for three years. While there she learned what is nameless and experienced a cultural healing. Convinced that this soul journey was something many in the Diaspora needed and could benefit from, she returned and began workshops with writers of varying degrees of abilities. The poetry produced led to a trip with some of those who participated in the Oakland workshop. There was an exchange with writers from Ghana in particular. Many of the poets were spoken word poets and they were challenged by written word poets. Inversely, academically trained poets were equally challenged by the spoken word tradition. This anthology lets these poets come together and share their poems in a way that expands both styles of poetry and poethood.

Vital to the anthology, inclusivity bolsters the collection because of the wide range of abilities, life experiences, and backgrounds of the poets assembled from Africa to the global Diaspora.

Complicating this laudable impetus to bring disparate voices and levels of experiences together in a single volume is the tension between poetry on the page; "Written Word" and the phenomena of "Spoken Word" on stage—is a reshaping of the idiom. What works on and off the page of navigating this tension.

Some of the points of interest show the ways in which collaboration occurs. The poems are linked in a Pan African approach with a Japanese poetry format, renshi, that interconnects words, themes, or phrases. The ways in which the writers worked together and shared makes this both a cultural and artistic work. In one poem the word "desert" is in a poem. It's very interesting how an African expresses this word and world of 'desert' and an African American. Language is a part of the rich way that this gathering of poets and poetry expands the experiences of both other writers and readers.

The notion of connections and identity with Africa was made a reality by Zoom and the trip to Ghana. This allowed people to see and feel the sand as well as meet artisans creating from local materials. These experiences all fed their imagination as they sought words to express the sounds of an African language, music, and people.

Much praise to those who conceived this collection and took the risk of cultural languages. Taking both subject and word choice, the poets embraced each other and shared a newly forged dialogue. This dialogue of Pan Africanism through the strategy of renshi, a Japanese form, creates a coming together of poets who share their words, thoughts and cultural lives from Africa to America. Melding (or not) African and African American syntax is challenging for the writers and the editors.

In many of the poems by African-born writers and African Americans, we see the contextualized remembering and homage to one's lineage is upended by language choices that reflect cultural differences and borrowing/melding.

For example, Alfred Nyagaka Nyamwange's "My Song, My Life" expresses an autobiographical narration: Nyamwange names his parents, their ages, and locates his home;

Two score and ten, mum Kerry
And dad Daudi were blessed with a son
This is my song, Alan, Oturi, born
In the green hills of Gusii land
Western Kenya, and grew in the village
Of Iteba, played in the village paths

Hide and seek in the banana groves
And corn patches, and threw sticks
And stones with village urchins,suffered
Injuries, left animals in our care to eat
Others' crops got beaten, collected firewood [...]

This graphic presentation of the locale is poetic and informative.
The language is simple and authentic. However later in the poem the
"borrowing" occurs:

Fetched from the springs
Where old women with tins and pots shovelled
Us to the edges and naughty girls spewed
On our faces, and with streaks of water
Sooty sufurias balanced on our heads
Chased by dogs, and mocked by fellas
From other hoods during string ball matches [...]

The writer goes back to his own vocabulary and continues to speak
to the school experience he had. His poetic language is dominant here,
but the borrowing of words such as "fellas" and "hoods" presents a jux-
taposition of time and place and helps the reader see the cross-cultural
exchanges that occur with the expansion of social media.

In the Diaspora, "Mefiri" by Chasejamison Akilah Manar-Spears,
Madam CJda3rd opens as such:

I was raised by the Deep
The dope, the spiraling, all-knowing flow of our mother: Ocean
Bled from the womb of our cosmic creatress
Breastfed stardust, rose quartz, and greatness
I'm an East Oakland Empress reborn each generation
I come from that powerful patience sustained by spiritual revelations.
Giving birth to our purposes feels as easy as lake walking.
Revolutionary talking, Black poetry reading, deep breathing, Afrikans
I come from knowing we belong together.
I come from the ocean.
From the dark side of the moon.
Where you can catch a glimpse of Yemoja and Oshun.

The poet uses a distant language and is non-autobiographical. There are more references to a heritage than immediately biological. This poem appears more verbal than the written. Terminology is a mix of slang and African cosmology. It suggests identity search and an assumed relationship with a past recalled in names rather than direct connection.

Here is the point at which the anthology editors needed to find a way to meld these two disparate poets. Renshi allows this to happen. By focusing on a theme and specific words, these two poems above speak with each other across syntactical, linguistic, and contextual differences. Sometimes, the African-born poet uses a vocabulary that is not organic to their culture and the African American poet relies on non-metaphoric expressions that may be a result that the origin of some words are not organic to their culture. Each comes to their work with words and experiences born out of histories that shape their choices of images and turn them into poetry. It is not the success or failure of this but rather, the boldness and courage to embrace and confront poetic structures, ideologies, and even language itself, in order to speak to one another. In this noble effort, each poetic pair—as well as this anthology as a whole—delivers.

The anthology is a culmination of workshops in Africa and America featuring the poets included, and shares experiences of foreigner/returnee, neo-African, borrower of phrases, and experimenter of styles that shape—and will continue to shape—the vibrant exchange between Africa and the Diaspora. Poetry is an artistic vehicle that allows this to happen with humility and pride; honesty and fear strive for a way to establish a meaningful dialogue after centuries of separation.

Biography Rashidah Ismaili

Poet, fiction writer, and playwright Rashidah Ismaili was born and raised in Dahomey, Benin. She earned a BFA in voice at the New York College of Music and an MA in social psychology at the New School for Social Research. She earned her PhD in ethnotherapy and psychodrama from the Herbert Holt Institute for Psychotherapy. She was active in the Black Arts Movement in New York City in the 1960s. Her poetry collections include Cantata for Jimmy (2004) and Missing in Action and Presumed Dead: Poems (1992). Ismaili coedited the anthology Womanrise (1978) and her work is included in The Heinemann Book of African Women's Poetry (1995). Composer Joyce Solomon-Moorman scored an opera, Elegies for the Fallen, based on Ismaili's poetry. It was performed in 2005 at the City University of New York's Borough of Manhattan Community College. A reading of Ismaili's own play, Rice Keepers, was staged in 2006 at the American Museum. In 2014, she published Autobiography of the Lower East Side: A Novel in Stories. For three decades, Ismaili has hosted Salon d'Afrique, a gathering for artists from Africa and the African Diaspora and Harlem residents. Her recent works include performing at the Harare International Fine Arts Festival (HIFA) in Zimbabwe, readings in Johannesburg and Pretoria, South Africa, inclusion in the historic New Daughters of Africa anthology, and producing the International Poetry Festival for Pen & Brush.

Introductory remarks from the founding director, Karla Brundage

In 2013, I was living in Cote d'Ivoire teaching English when the principal, Daphne Neal, encouraged all the teachers to attend the African International Schools Association (AISA) conference. It was there that I met Sir Black, co-founder of Ehalakasa, a poetry collective of young Ghanaian poets. Sir Black was in the midst of creating what is now the "slam poetry" culture in Accra. That year, I invited him to Abidjan to talk to my students about how the oral or griot tradition of West Africa inspired the spoken word tradition in the United States. Sir Black and I spent many hours discussing how, after 400 years in which many people of the African Diaspora have been subject to either enslavement or colonial rule, we both came to Hip-hop as a way to teach self-empowerment and to bring voice to Black youth in the Diaspora.

Unfortunately the next year, the Ebola pandemic hit West Africa and we were unable to host any more exchanges on the continent. My father became ill and I moved back to the U.S. in 2016, but I kept in touch with Sir Black. After a few years of planning, we launched the first exchange. By this time, I was attending Mills College to complete my MFA in poetry as a Community Engagement Fellow. With the support of both Mills and Ehalakasa, the idea of West Oakland to West Africa came to fruition. What I did not know was the impact that this exchange would have on all the participants. After the exchange with the support of Pacific Raven Press, we published our first book, *Our Spirits Carry Our Voices* and then we traveled to Ghana where we paticipated in a poetry slam with Ehalakasa and our partners. We also went to the Cape Coast and Elmina where we visited the slave dungeons and this was a powerful moment for all of us. The power of that Sankofa moment—that return to our ancestors—forever changed us.

Sankofa is an Akan Twi word that means "to retrieve," but the meaning of Sankofa is more broadly expanded upon in this Akan proverb: "Se wo were fi na wosankofa a yenkyi." Translated from the Akan language, this proverb essentially means, "it is not taboo to go back and fetch what you forgot." This word came into my consciousness when I saw the 1993 film *Sankofa* directed by Haile Gerima, which focused on the Atlantic slave trade. The impact of this film cannot be understated and the guiding symbol was a Sankofa bird that flies from the slave ship, symbolizing a return to Africa, to learn its true heritage and rich history.

After the success of the first exchange, Koku Konu of Cultural Intellectual Association in Lagos, Nigeria, reached out to me to see if his group of poets could participate in an exchange. We engaged in several readings and events with them and they produced the first book. We hosted the second exchange in which twenty-six poets including ayodele nzinga, first Poet Laureate of Oakland, California, participated and experienced a workshop on narrative poetry. Our groups are composed of students and elders, as well as emerging and published poets. We have also been able to include folks with neurodivergent styles as well as differently-abled people. While I was working with Mills College and while our group welcomed folks of all races, much of my vision has been to create a safe space for Black people to engage across the Diaspora and in this way, over 95% of the participants in our exchanges identify as Black.

To this day, we have done four poetry exchanges. Two were with a group called Cultural Intellectual Association, or CIA_Lagos, in Nigeria. One poetry exchange was with poets in Ghana, as well as our current exchange with Kisii University in Kisii, Kenya. The current exchange which was supported by Cal Humanities includes fifty-four poets from Oakland, Kenya, and Nigeria. CIA_Lagos is directed by Koku Konu who, after hearing about our program, reached out to me and invited West Oakland to West Africa to participate in an exchange inspired by the poetry of Christopher Okigo, a famous Nigerian poet. We then agreed to begin an exchange with poets from West Oakland. About the same time, I had been working with Kim McMillon who is editing the anthology *Black Fire this Time*. Through this collaboration, as well as through poet Rashidah Ismaili of Harlem's Salon d'Afrique, I was introduced to Christopher Okemwa, of Kisii University and editor of the international poetry anthology *I Can't Breathe*. Dr. Okemwa gathered a number of students and we began an exchange with the hopes of attending the Kistrech International Poetry Festival that was a little over a year away.

The key to this exchange succeeding is the curriculum and the format. On the incubation process of this project, I had envisioned a program that aligned closely with Youth Speaks. I had hoped to create a Brave New Voices version in Africa. However, when I got to Mills my professors asked me, "Do you really think you can do this?" There is something inside of me that loves a challenge and while I doubted I could logistically host a poetry slam festival in Ghana, I did not want to give up on the idea of an artist exchange. It was in a lucid moment one night when my ancestors spoke to me. For ten years, I had been exchanging poetry using a format called renshi, shared with me by my heart-friend, Allison Francis, in Hawaii, where I grew up. Renshi is an epistolary form in which a pair of writers, usually close friends, exchanges poetry in letter form using the last line of their partner's poem to begin their own. It was at this moment, when my ancestors spoke to me, that I saw how the project could come to life—despite the obstacles of distance and time. The renshi form (which translated means linked or chained together) became the foundation of the exchanges. In each exchange, I matched pairs of poets who wrote for several weeks on different themes, engaged in writing workshops, and used the renshi form to facilitate connections. The result was mind-blowing. Authentic connections were formed and the chain actually caused a reaction of growth and cultural healing between both partners.

It is a simple form, but poetry is a catalyst for the journal back to our past and into the future. It is an Afro-Futuristic time machine in which our participants can share stories, which in turn, allows for us to heal throughout the African Diaspora.

Acknowledgments

I want to first thank the ancestors who have opened a path I did not previously imagine. Who was to know that in 1993, while pregnant with my daughter, Asha Jade Amenu Brundage-Moore, that I would encounter the movie *Sankofa*.

Through this encounter with the imagination, and with the blessing of many more mistakes and trials, my own experience would lead me on a similar journey. Without the ancestors, without the planting the seed and the watering of the roots, the tree may not have blossomed.

Thank you also to my mother, Kathryn Waddell Takara, poet, brilliant woman, traveler, teacher and inspiration. Her journey on Crossroads Africa just years before I was born allowed her to envision bridges she has always been building.

Many thanks to the poets who participated in this book, giving their time and energy to meet and share their hearts. Thank you especially to San Francisco Poet Laureate, Tongo Eisen-Martin for connecting me with DonJuan Carter-Woodard, Landon Smith, and the talented folks at Patrice Lumumba Writing Collective. Thank you to Wanda Sabir for holding the Maafa Commemoration for over thirty years, for being a mentor of full warrior womanhood, for holding space for ancestors, and for her willpower that always says yes, before saying no.

The publishers of this book Elyssar Press have been so generous in this endeavor and thank you to Allie Rigby, our editor, for all her hard work on this manuscript.

I also need to thank our partners, Cultural Intellectual Association of Lagos led by the fearless Koku Konu who helped organize our poets in Nigeria. Thank you also to Christopher Okemwa, Professor and Founding Director of Kistrech Poetry Festival, for organizing his students at University of Kenya, Kisii, to participate.

The exchange itself had many supporters and helpers including Meg Piece, Administrative Assistant; Tyrice Deane Brown, Content Curator; Petrut Ababei, Web Designer; Oakland Poet Laureate, ayodele nzinga, workshop leader. Thank you to Shuffle Collective for hosting our readings and to Tess Bliven specifically for creating our video. Many thanks to Oakland Cultural Fund and Cal Humanities Quick Grant for their immense support as well.

PART ONE:
Kisii, Kenya to East Oakland

DISPUTED AREA

ETHIOPIA

MOYALE

MARSABIT

WAJIR

MAKUTANO

KITALE

MARALAL

KIMILILI

UNGOMA   ELDORET

ISIOLO

KAKAMEGA

YA   ELDAMARAVINENYAHURURU   KENYA

KISUMUMUHORONI

MOLONAKURUJOL KALOU

KERICHO   NYERI   GARISSA

MABAY   GIUGIL   KERUGOYAEMBU

Kisii

NAIVASHA

WEND   MARAGUA

IGORI   NAROK   THIKA   MWINGI

EHANCHA   RUIRU

NAIROBI   KITUI

ATHI RIVER

MACHAKOS

MALINDI

ANIA   TAVETA

KIFI

MARIAKAN

MOMBASA

I. Chase & Alfred

My Song, My Life

by Alfred Nyagaka Nyamwange

Two score and ten, mum Kerry
And dad Daudi were blessed with a son
This is my song, Alan, Oturi, born
In the green hills of Gusii land
Western Kenya, and grew in the village
Of Iteba, played in the village paths
Hide and seek in the banana groves
And corn patches, and threw sticks
And stones with village urchins, suffered
Injuries, left animals in our care to eat
Others' crops got beaten, collected firewood
From the corn fields, the straws and hurled
Sticks at dry blue gum trees, stole guavas
And ripe maize to roast, and sugar cane.
Fetched from the springs
Where old women with tins and pots shovelled
Us to the edges and naughty girls spewed
On our faces, and with streaks of water
Sooty sufurias balanced on our heads
Chased by dogs, and mocked by fellas
From other hoods during string ball matches
We had fights with Mauritius thorn pods and
Sticks and watched rams square it out
On the plains amidst tall and swamped patches.

And school saved me from those talons
And at Mokoro primary I found
The pics and colours of glossy books
Too attractive, I remained and wrote on slates
Sat on logs and stones until I grew lanky,
And in this I discovered worlds of books
Of lands afar, simplified series of Dickens,
Shakespeare, Twain etc. and got fixated

Until at Kiomosh secondary, I discovered
The Achebe, Ngugi, Amadi magic
I read books, I imbibed knowledge
And saw myself get a high school slot
In the prestigious Gas school and my next stop
Was UON for Bachelors, Political science and
English and finally detoured into teaching.

Over three decades, I've stuck to that chalk
With a passion to shape the youth.
How great to inspire, plant and grow humanity!
At least that's me, son of Daudi.

Mefiri

by Chasejamison Akilah Manar-Spears, Madam CJda3rd

I was raised by the Deep
The dope, the spiraling, all-knowing flow of our mother: Ocean
Bled from the womb of our cosmic creatress
Breastfed stardust, rose quartz, and greatness
I'm an East Oakland Empress reborn each generation
I come from that powerful patience sustained by spiritual revelations.
Giving birth to our purposes feels as easy as lake walking,
Revolutionary talking, Black poetry reading, deep breathing, Afrikans
I come from knowing we belong together.
I come from the ocean.
From the dark side of the moon
Where you can catch a glimpse of Yemoja and Oshun.
Feeling the juice drip out of a taco truck masterpiece
Radically reclaimed histories spray painted on these streets
Mystical femme mystique pouring libations over beats
An everlasting line of ancestral memories, gracefully reminding me
who the fuck I am
I will always be that duality, divinity, destiny reclaiming everything
I come from the most high
God took their divine time
Painting and sustaining just exactly where I come from
They stay tryna deny us children of the sun
As our vessels radiate the restorative truth that we are one
The time has come
To remember the love we are from.

Baba Moraa, Matriarch Moraa

by Alfred Nyagaka Nyamwange

To return to the love we are from, I recall
That toothy smile and protruding teeth
Light laugh skin lines that made your beauty
And sonorous voice that exuded a warmth
In your expanse wrappers with stretched arms
Like a massive wall, you stood before us,
Me, a rock, to bar the wind,the rains,the
Leeches, your warm body, a fountain from
Which resuscitation, straw of my want,
I drew sustenance, sap, to live and stand tall,
And warm my hands.

The smell of fresh dung and soil, baby vomit
Roast meat, like a perfume, pervaded our
Beings, with saturation, as your hands cupped
Around my mouth, gruel poured, fingers
Directed it down my throat, in gulps
I swallowed, my flailing hands, weakened, until
My belly like a vessel, swollen like a ball you
Planted me in a banana shade as you worked
In the shamba, I rolled in mud, too fed to cry!

Baba Moraa, Matriarch Moraa
Your rough hands washed me off scabies
In dark brown herbs and roots whose bitter tea
I drank to kill the worms, to dissipate the ills.
Your toothy smile egging me on, I drunk
I sucked blood tipped soft veges, sour milk

And ugali baked and burnt characteristically
A favourite grandchild that you spoiled
Pampered me, made me a prince, to sing
My song of my childhood,to tell the world
How special you were,we were to you!

You would be gone for ages but not your
Deeds that live in us, me, as I stride the world.

Ancestresses

by Chasejamison Akilah Manar-Spears, Madam CJda3rd

"God is my first ancestor." -Destiny Muhammad

*This poem is dedicated to Henrietta Lacks & all my divine feminine
ancestors*

The world rotates around the sun of Black womanhood. Literally...
we blessed.

By feminine ancestry
Hood alchemy
Slowly cooked greens.

I don't always know the meanings of my ancestor's names... I am so
forever grateful for
The blessings they send me either way.
The mercy and the grace
The pure beauty in our face
As we balance and raise
Make mistakes to rematriate.

I give thanks
In every language known and unknown
For the women whose names
We rarely say.

II. Landon & Josephat

Where Love Grows on Trees

by Josephat Ndege Mauti

I come from a place
Where love grows on trees
Yet no one is permitted to pick.
Roses hang down from roofs
But cursed are you if you dare smell any.
Honey flows down the mountains, but
Alas, you can't lick it even if it trickles down to your lips.

I come from a place
Where life is better lived in a dream
Women see their husbands once in a blue moon.
A place where hunters are often hunted
Security officers–insecure.

I come from a place
Where music booms at the dawn of dusk
Roads impassable at sundown
And mothers rush for the 6 p.m. TV series.
Yes, I come from a place
Where all roads lead homeward at dusk
For home is always the best place.

Broken Home

by Landon Smith

For home is always the best place
to find where liberation was stolen;
if you can see past the smoke from headboard bullet holes
    Good bones break just as easily if the CIA stages a coup on time
    Just to make it home in time for imperialism to be celebrated by
    not asking questions.
Maybe America was the broken home Gil was coming from
Dirt beneath fingernails won't come clean with blood mixed in from Iraqi
floors
seeing just enough grieving to displace a generation with bombed buildings
to call home.
    And Oval Office regime changes
    passing torches in ceremony over the bodies
    just melanated enough to be not human enough for home to
    be breath.
For home to be more than
a lost country determined to eat itself.

A Powerful Woman

by Josephat Ndege Mauti

A lost country determined to eat itself
founded the extreme situations, dear Rose.
Back ever bent,
tilling and toiling.
You were a bulldozer;
turned upside down
the mounds of mud
to bake the diet of the day.

With your sweat, dear Rose,
you scented our household
now, rose flowers grow everywhere.
Thank you, dear Rose,
you're our Hero.

Neal and Be Seen

by Landon Smith

You're our Hero
   spoken to puddles on funeral pamphlets
Flower arrangements cannot negotiate peace
   for my great grandmother's goodbyes

History handed me family remains in obituary scans
   Told me to pray and be saved by fable
I picture her in my hallucinations sometimes
   Bienville backwoods in her palm pulse
   Humid skin gripping bible leather for hope

   Teardrops on southern soil I never knew about
   Watered roots from the nerve endings she felt deadened
Talk to me, mama
Sing the tales of survival your suitcase couldn't fit
Oklahoma dust on my eulogy clipping
   I'm clutching Polaroid photocopies
   to a casket story two smiles from Vallejo migration
   Enough LA in my walk to find you Bienville bootprint free
Twelve branches past Pomona saltwater
  Might see you in my next negotiation for peace

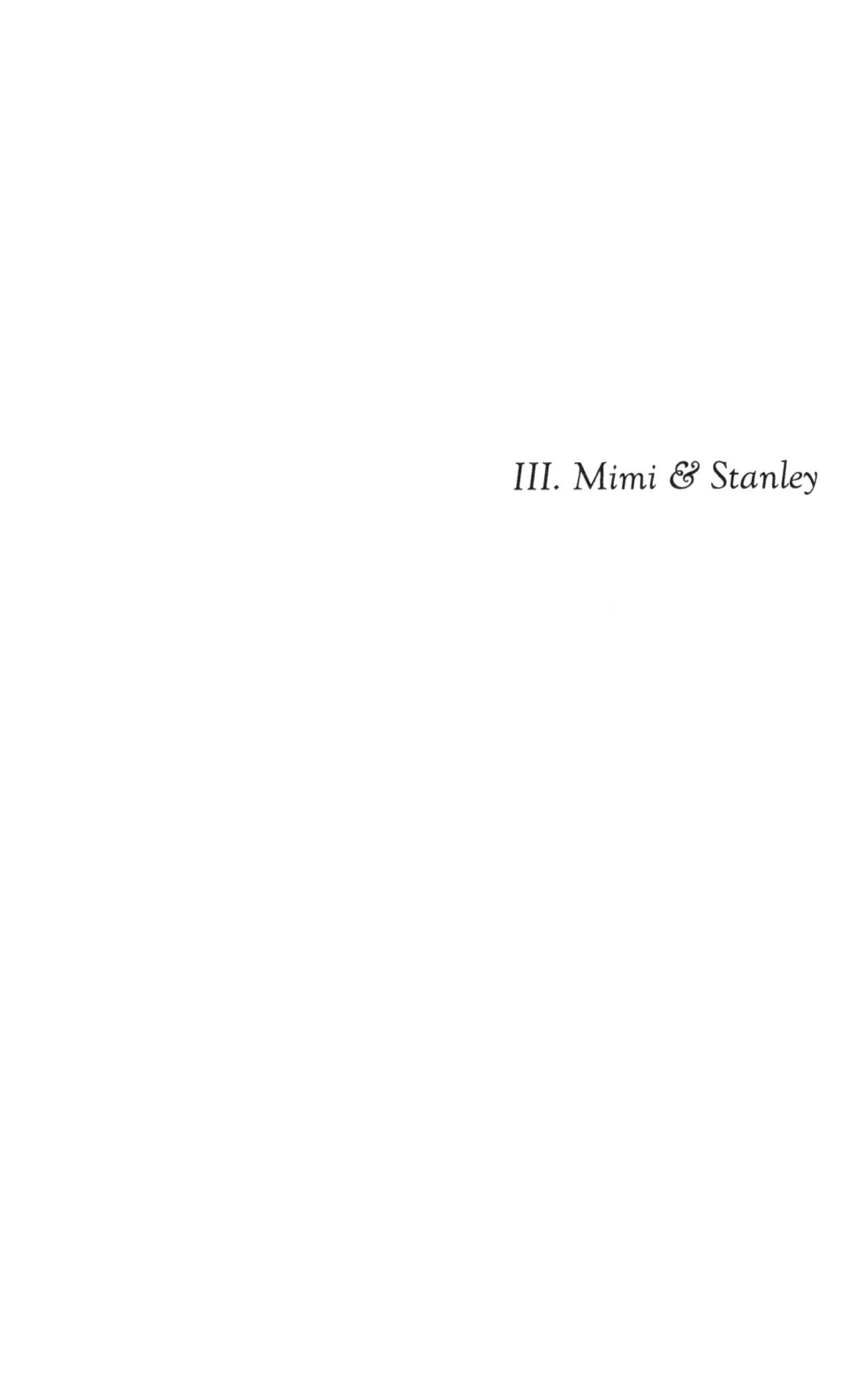

III. Mimi & Stanley

Shards

by Stanley Kipkorir Chemweno

The pain in my past
My youth is dotted with shards of glass
Each serves to remind me the years of pain and scars
Over the years my emotions have matured
My tears no longer rent the atmosphere
I'm human yes but the scabs have long healed
I'm me because I was strong for me
Through thick and thin
I've met the forces of life head on
And many times a victor I've become

Of Twisted Galaxies

by Mimi Tempestt

Many times a victor I've become
Allowing my fists to open up and expose my palms
I deliver bravery, humble to my desires
I speak with a mouthful of twisted galaxies on my tongue
Blessings that become a whirlpool of stars
& planets
& stardust
& half-bitten moons
& dark matter
Bending a prism of light to radiate through our lustful souls
When was the last time you loved like the universe whispered
free in your ear?
When was the last dream where you shed these makeshift bones,
Testified that a body is a small cup of this universe's river?
How do you begin your being: from the beginning or the end?

I dreamt in sunflowers today
Let the rays coo love all the way up my spine
Twisted into a fistful of emotions, a rainbow serpent
Sliding about this earth as protector of my wildest memories
How do you pronounce your soul: As dark or light?
I am pink, in theory
Originally red, bursting like millions of conjoined suns
I am all that God is and will ever become

Influential Woman

by Stanley Kipkorir Chemweno

She is a woman
a black woman with a bright smile
Confidence oozes from her effortlessly
yet her industriousness matches no other
Speaks eloquently and dorns stylishly

I yearn for her dreams
of positivity and civilization
She speaks and they listen
words of wisdom and enlightenment

She knows her rights
but fights for that of others
She wields power with gentleness
a woman of substance I say

An intelligent and open-minded persona
Cares for the weak
and provides shelter in her heart
for the homeless and lost
She is a force to reckon
and a soul to call upon
an influential woman

She Makes Beautiful

by Mimi Tempestt

an influential woman's withering bones light up the path of my life
in this state of decay
she makes beautiful
all that she can
running in our veins
are our mother's dreams, long gone

                                                   in this state of decay
           she makes beautiful
       a wish for life, brand new
         her prayers act as halos
       her mistakes act as lessons

her youth
flying south
migrating in a cloudy ethos
its wings, dusted
a potential burned low

                             in this state of decay
            she makes beautiful
the greyish tint that haunts her hair
                a smile,
           dim lit with fire
      there are whispers of life
      that she did not let grow

in this state of decay
she makes beautiful
all that she can
which isn't much
the precision
of her love

when magnified and seen in our blood

lights the entirety of a universe
nebulas and stars
that have collapsed
and died in her mind
she gives
birth to new galaxies
that reside in us

IV. adrienne & Kelvin

I Am a Person

by Kelvin Kombo Motuka

I am a person
Doing much under table
With a lot of quietness
Lending an eye
To those seeing no value in I

I am a person
Believing in humble steps
Little dreams
Embracing hope, that little dreams are huge

I am a person
Beginning life solely
Carrying on even when
I know not
Its destination

I am a person
Opening wide satellite bands
On either side of cheek
Gathering, but with a sieve
Knowing that wit flows
Even from a mouth
Considered trash

I am a person
Wiring all my senses
Direct to the inner voice
Knowing conscience is Central
Processing Unit
Detector, indicator
Monitor and communicator

Heart in Hand - *Iman Gibson*

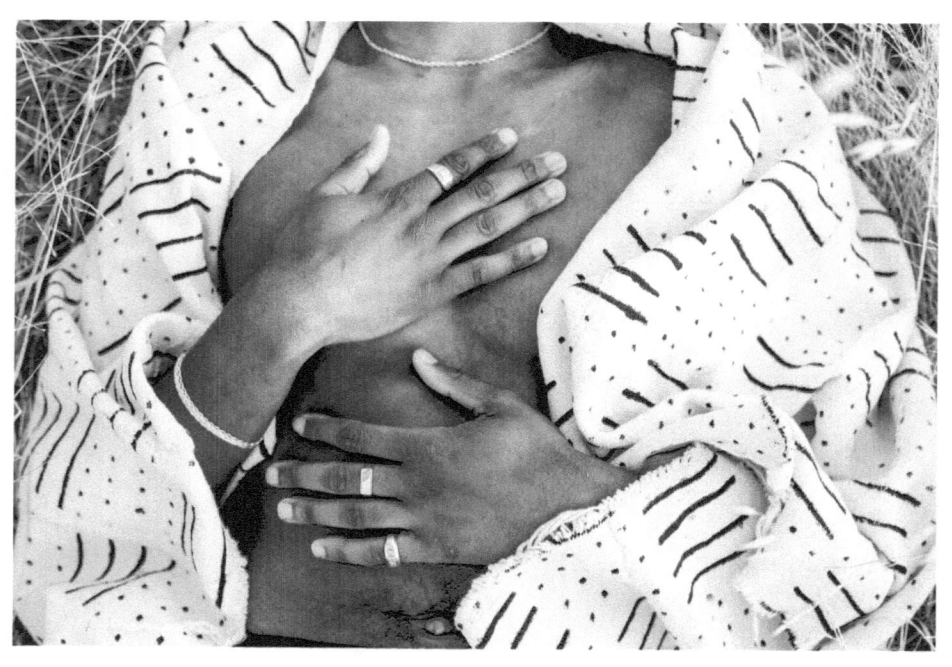

Wine

by adrienne danyelle oliver

To age gracefully
a grape must surrender skin
and embrace the wait

And Embrace the Wait

by Kelvin Kombo Motuka

Embrace the wait
Hold tight
Cling to patience like it were wild grass

To wait lends sight
Begets faith
Optimism for better

Celebration and jubilation
Verily, products of wait
As you endure
Amid stumbling blocks

Mumble not
Walk meticulously
Stepping stones
Up the ladder

At most opportune moment
Wait sires pleasantries
Clearing mess and way paving
For success

home/body

by adrienne danyelle oliver

I remember bricks
                    the color of cement
a moss-covered foundation
                         charcoal rooftop shingles
steel gutters
                peeling paint on a porch railing
a window box with
                    just dirt in it
                a golf course within
walking distance
I can see my first house
so clearly now
          there's shadow over it
I'm the sunshine that cast it to the
ground
          this is more story than poem
about the body I had to become
for sun to let me shape[shift] shadows
I had to learn that we are all one
delusion of home
          a paycheck away from...
          nursing a knife-in-the-back injury...
          our arms wound tight around
          the baby that died
                         in utero
and passed through the opening left for birthing
dreams
          we signed away   the birth canal for a fixed term interest rate
with low interest in our promise
we put our overgrown bodies into a baskenette
became a floating down river to...
what a beautiful target we'd become

shot bullseye dead into the center of the body

I remember owning a home
          if owning is the right word
for signing a 30-year mortgage
I had at least bought into a dream
the same one
          so many other Americans agree to as
                              being real
                    the realest thing is
a property line
          I didn't quite understand what a surveyor was
—I was 22 years old—
          A man came around marking my land
putting wooden stakes
          in the ground with orange flags tied
around them
          My dream was marked off from the
          sewage line in the front to the wire fence in the
backyard
          I didn't know what it meant then to pay attention
to the neighbor's yard
or to drive through
                    the neighborhood at night
I crossed the threshold
          with a poor woman's desire
not knowing what I do

...

Mama, forgive me for forgetting that home is
my feet in the grass

my skin in the sun
my toes in the sand
Now, I am a decaying American
dream
How was I supposed to know that the American part
was the cancer?
...

these days I find home
in
space between breaths
in line breaks
in pauses between pen strokes
in hard returns
Miles Davis
home is not outside this heart
these acres in my chest
put all 40 delusions to rest
      home
home   home
      is here
I own this home
          deed signed by my next breath
me
      home
body
      poem
story

V. LadiRev & Becca the Poet

From Desert to Dreams

by Becca the Poet

Full of life and great exposure
But I grew up in a desert
Where living conditions were hostile
The sand dunes were my pillow
The food tasted joyless
Crows called out in their horrible voices
Soap trees stared silently at the sun
The land was flat and barren
The desert lions were more furious than before
My tongue was swollen from lack of water
Everything smelled burned and blasted
At the age of seven
We settled in a better environment
With greener pastures
Tadam! It was a new day's dawn
It was a pinch of hope, a dime of perplexity
My dreams recovered
I got to school
And that's when I developed my writing skills
Reflected on society

I Come From

by LadiRev

Reflected from society, I learned at an early age fate is never destined
I come from patched fences and hand-me-down blankets
Southern hospitality raised me to be a servant to adversity but
California air
Warps you into a martyr
You would think the land be desert because of the salty water but
Evolution served us better
My father's father traveled north lookin for freedom
He found law instead
My grandmother was banished from New York, this led her West
I was created from a clash of cultures
Cognitive dissonance and order
Furious lions wait in police cars on corners
But there is still love
Grown babies raised by elders twice removed
Teenagers dressing battle wounds
Everyday we wake to conquer

When I Grow Up

by Becca the Poet

Lawns have always stood beautiful
For she who nurtures it is still careful
Her efforts never run in vain
She always alters blessings all along
It always tickles my senses
Just like the fragrance of a rose
That there is a soul that treasures me
Upholds me and soothes my soul
She is like the flowers that sprout out high
and stars that twinkle during the night
She is my small idol
My sweet honeybunch
She likes calling me out
When doing some chores
Just to show me how to do it
So when I grow up I don't depart from it
It's the beauty of a woman
When I grow up
I want to be like her
That's my mom

Back Den

by LadiRev

Then he found the dove, it was his time to rest
Back in the day my feets knew ground like dust knows air
I'd grip grass between my toes to shake hands with her
Little pebbles and stones mixed with rocks and sand be good training
Ground
We didn't know that we was playing with freedom
Our souls danced on sun-kissed roads
Every day was a journey
Tree marks cemented on ankles
Steady eyes can see heritage in these folds, culture in the arch
My momma's voice echoing jives
Back den flesh touched flesh
Tired bones rested on plastic couches
And air spoke honestly of the earth
I never knew innocence but we knew we were pure
Back before way back when imagination dictated socialism
When money was on trees in everybody backyard
Snowflakes made heavenly icees
More caterpillars than butterflies cause struggle gave peace
And now, full body and settled mind, just wishing to be a kid again

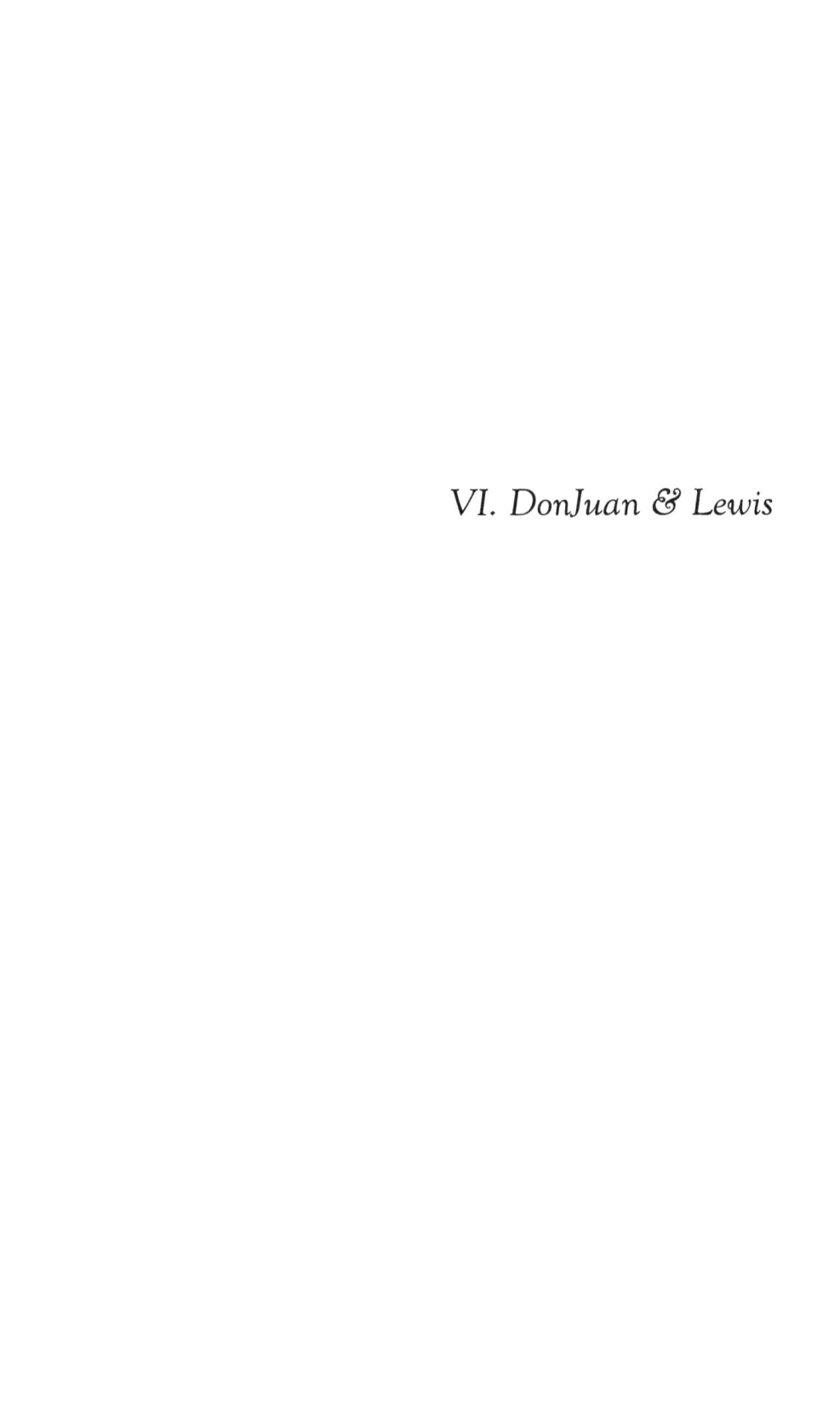

VI. DonJuan & Lewis

Nia Wilson

by DonJuan Carter-Woodard

At every dawn the cock crows
We all sat and watched
No audio needed but I can only imagine
The pure terror
No one said all Angels have peaceful transitions
Martyrs are not always willing participants
Our women
Daughters
Granddaughters
Sisters, mothers, grandmothers
Can you see the terror of the screen
Although the sound is absent you still hear
The screams
Notice how no one came to their aid
The hate from a man the world deems
Mentally unfit
But I guess when your skin is black they feel you ain't worth shit
And the perpetrator is white
Aww that poor boy was just sick
Reverse the narrative and you know what you get
This young woman is now my ancestor
Held in my head with the highest regard
For it's a reminder placed next to so many thousand others
That my moral fabric is scared
We watch this happen in our faces and they tell us
Exactly who they think we are
Not a human being in need of justice
But another N-I-G-G-E-R
This is for the young lady who was cut down in her youth
For a soul that watches over us from beyond the stars
For the family that carries this weight daily
Just know that your pain is also ours

I wish I could speak of a woman that accomplished great heights
But I can't ever get rid of the family's faces I seen on the news that night
This is to my ancestor Nia Wilson
Yet younger than me she may be
Because if they let an atrocity like this happen to this teenage girl
What the fuck you think they'll let happen to me
Anyone with eyes can see
The blind watch the news every day
No matter how much we march
We can't take this hatred away
So in the attempt to honor her we still say her name
Because if was my daughters that went through this on that platform
I'd want you to do the same

I Wish You Were Here

by Lewis Wamwanda

I'd want you to do the same
To watch the twinkling stars
The shining moon
To hold on to our memories
Tears stinging your eyes
When I leave for good

Now as I sit by your grave
I laugh amidst tears
Of how we used to play under the sky
I miss you

I wish you were here
To listen to the songs of my youth
I have a lot to share,
Still I keep your warm sheet

I wish you were here
To wet my lips with your kisses
To play your favorite song
Tell me how beautiful I am

I am married to your grave
Prepare a way for my coming
Prepare your hands for a hug
I wish you were here
Then you'll soothe me to sleep

What happened to our dreams?
Of you marrying me
Of me giving you a son and daughter
You shattered our dreams
But still I wish you were here

I wish you were here
To cuddle me under your warmth
To make me laugh with your silly jokes
You were funny, you know
These days I cry myself to sleep

I Remember

by DonJuan Carter-Woodard

These days I cry myself to sleep
Carpet
I remember this carpet
Multicolored
Blue in composition
Bed for this young boy
Housed in a studio apartment on Seminary Ave.
Vast enough for a growing preteen

Foil
I remember aluminum foil
The fear and intrigue of it
Made to store food but for me
This is barrier
Rats cannot chew through aluminum foil
Or at least that's what mama says

This carpet
Only shared by my family when the thunder rings outside
Thunder seems to come more frequent on summer days
Holes in the building let you know
Lightning might not strike in the same place twice
But dammit it gets close sometimes

Stamps
I remember stamps
The same anxiety gave my mother
This book of stamps for her mental degradation
For me it meant Doritos lunchmeat and Kool-aid packets
I remember I was in charge of the stamps
Also meaning
I was in charge of bringing home the list of groceries

Candles
I always remember candles
I always seen candles
On those no light nights
Storytime sounds better when the TV isn't working
I guess the whole neighborhood feels the same
These candles on the corner have been lit for days
Stories are told by drunken bystanders
Only time then I remember seeing grown men cry

Stains
I remember the stains in the concrete
Where pools of blood took time to soak
Remember walking around the stains
In an attempt to not aggravate the ghost

Music
I remember the music
Mama hates the way it makes the house shake
The vibration resonates in my soul
Drums make me remember a feeling
Can't explain it really
But I remember it feels like home
It's funny how this transition sticks in my mind

Potatoes
Potatoes and rice
Easy meals for a weary family
After hours on AC transit
82L or the 57
40L or the 72
Numbers I will always remember

Urine
I remember the smell of urine
Tucked off in corners
Corner slept in by the less fortunate
Makes me appreciate that carpet
Never knowing these nights would structure my future days

Survival
I remember survival
Bruises from North Oakland Carter Middle School days
The two-hour bus ride back to East Oakland
After the barrage of fist and feet

Respect
I remember respect
The want of it
The fight for it
The demand for it
These are normal days for kids my age
The environment that grew us to be

Invincible
I remember feeling invincible
Which is an upgrade from the days of being invisible
Knowing that time is ether that drifts away
But memory is solid and concrete

Muscle memory
These memories are strong
Chipping pieces off of this statue
The masterpiece of God like energy
I call me

Where I Come From, Where I Call Home

by Lewis Wamwanda

They call me Wamwanda Lewis,
In this place that I call home
This humble place with humble people
The place my ancestors lived
My grandparents grew
My parents were born
The place I call home

The pride of our homeland
The pride of our blood, our culture
These that never cease to amaze me
The isikuti dances, the isikuti dancers
The way they shake their shoulders

The obusuma and ingoho
Aha! The pride of our food
That which represents our culture
That which makes us be the Abaluyha
Ingoho, say no more, Obhusuma
Our food, our culture

I come from the Abaluyha
The people from western Kenya
Those who dance the mulongo
The songs of the young men
The beautiful songs of initiation
The pride of our culture
The pride of our men

Have you ever seen bull fights?
The place I call home, the place I come from
We have bull fights, bull fighting is our pride
From far and wide we converge
We sing and dance
Eat and drink, haa, the liquor we call busaa
Our pride, our culture

Nafula and Wafula our pride
Nekesa and Wekesa our people
The Abaluyha we are
The men and women of Ingoho
We are the Obusuma people
And we are amazing
The place I come from, the place I call home

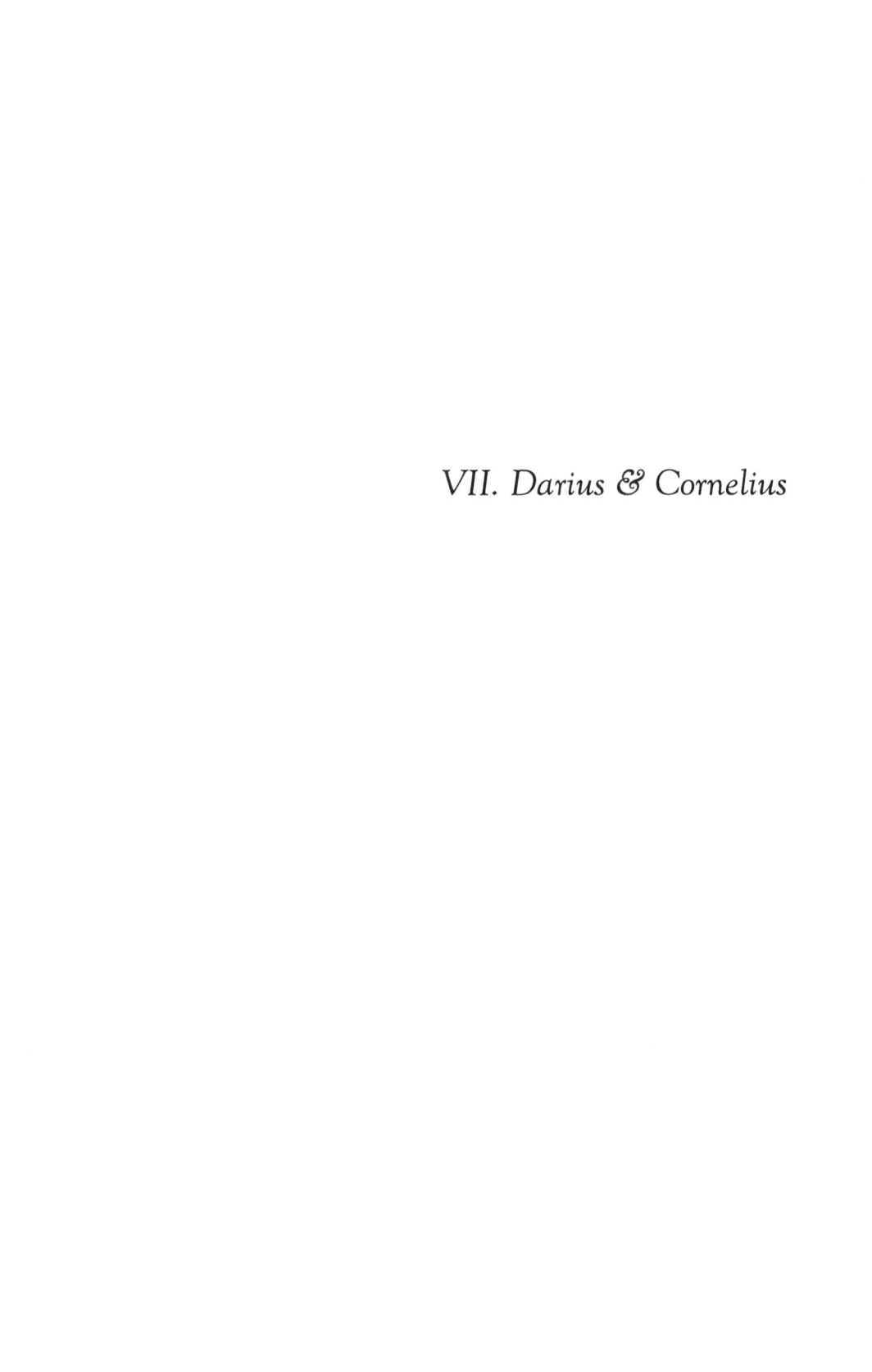

VII. Darius & Cornelius

I Am From

by Cornelius Kipkosgei

I am from
The blowy streets of Dalan
The winds brush kisses on my cheeks
And raindrops tremble on the wood and glass
I feel like a lamb, its knees: skinned and bruised.

I am from
The other side of life
Tomorrow holds my faint hopes
I stand between life and death
Yet where I am, nothing stands.

I am from
Far, beyond the plains
In the midst of crowded strangers
Yesterday it was me, today I am a stranger to myself
I am from where the blazing ball reminds me of "me."

Blame

by Darius Simpson

i am from where a blazing ball reminds me of me
but i live on the first East side of my life
clumps of hair skipping over sidewalk cracks
tire tracks from sideshow scrapes making a mural of the intersection
a city of tremors and zip codes shaken loose from the hands of its natives
colonialism don't respect its own rules
all's fair in genocide except self defense
there are humans too close to squalor
or squalor too close to wallets that could solve the contradiction
there's empty baby bottles under the freeway
there's brand new cop cars patrolling decade-old encampments
dead grass grappling with the distance between beating hearts
and piles of repurposed furniture and court papers drifting toward gutters
climate crisis confused about how many people we let pile up outdoors
while profits skyrocket for empty housing units
while a high rise crawls out the chapped lips of an investor
but i'm not really sure how leasing works
i got my degree in human decency
i'm not really up on the latest ethics for ownership
all my comrades keep space on the couch and a spare blanket
push the limits of a 4-door honda civic and there's always enough to share
there's always a good excuse to shoplift under capitalism
there's always sufficient evidence to start fires inside empire
i'm not sure what's legal and what's tradition anymore
at some point sick of this shit should lead us to get rid of city leaders
lest we be made of plastic promises too

i blame the suffering last for how they survive the winter
i blame the president for rainy days
i blame poverty on the police
i blame international military occupations on police
i blame police for all the times my father bit his tongue on the job
i blame police for my lazy eye twitch and my obsessive desire to produce
i blamed the sheriff's office last week when i stubbed my toe
and it left a star-shaped blood stain in my sock.

I Had a Sweet Breast

by Cornelius Kipkosgei

And it left a star-shaped blood stain in my sock
To remind me of a gloomy, dark night:
Crimson milk oozed from her pores
The frozen night sucked her warm breaths
Depths of her soul sank beneath beds of sand.

She left behind a little nest for her young love
The walls of clay remind me of yesteryears
I hear echoes of her dulcet hums enticing the night
The clatter of dishes and utensils remind me of her
I, a lad, stared at glasses sitting on the shelves.

A mat dotted with stars lie on the doorstep
It makes me think of her artistic, gentle hands:
Painted roses at the backyard on the bricks
Caressed my senses with petals of lavender
And held the little me under a blanket of serenity.

Her ruby lips taught me lifetime lessons
Told me not to lie, unless I have to
Told me to fight, and know when to back down
Told me to be strong, yet a tear still drops for her
I had a sweet breast.

Last Call

by Darius Simpson

i say i need to drink less and tonight is the third night in a row that my left hand is a short glass of whiskey. does that make me a liar, or an escape artist? and does it really make a difference on a san francisco sunday where the shoreline is coughing up hazmat suits? haze of unclearing throats meandering toward a bluepinkgold pacific backdrop. N95 means more to civilians now than it should. election season means we may not make it to the ballot and perhaps this disaster was man-made. perhaps if we had emptied more magazines in the right direction there would be less obituary on the east side this morning. my therapist who is neither licensed nor a therapist speaks fluent empty shot glass. exchanges horror stories from the work week across a wooden countertop confessional. asks, what you runnin' from? i say, you right, pour another one and watch me never run anywhere again. either it goes down gasoline or ice water. either way our session ends with my legs stuttering into a dancefloor. to be clear, after two drinks anywhere my left foot lands is a dancefloor and i'm floating toward the sweet spot in the crowd where bent knees begat spiraling backs. where sweat is offered up in praise to the DJ's intuition. hooked elbow swung around the neck of my new best friend who was a stranger 30 seconds ago. until that one song when the entire venue faded to background noise while we—gods of salted skin, uncles who inherited the groove from our grandfathers, backyard two-step practitioners challenged by what you know bout this?! and trained to kill that shit—fastened our eyes on the precision of each other's poplock. mirrored lean with rock and harlem shake with dougie. one of us cast an ayyyyeee! spell while the other spun the floor into red velvet. twisted the air into a thanksgiving kitchen humid. liquor has a funny way of ironing the wrinkles out of introductions. so 3 or 4 hours or shots or bathroom breaks in there we were bouncing limbs in the middle of no one's living room. for a split second thought we might've been immortal if we just drank enough midnight. if we absorbed enough brown elixir. but we know what moonlight does to Black functions when the music stops. what uniformed wolves linger beyond the overwhelming exchange between bass drum and ear drum. how quickly the end of a song can bleed into a more lasting quiet. happy endings are for white women. glass slippers were invented by white men. glass slippers make for a messy dance floor. glass slippers make it hard to run from sirens.

VIII. Dee Allen. & Evans

Resident

by Dee Allen.

Not a native, but a resident
Of my corner of East Oakland

Where poverty dominates,
Where broke-on-broke crime
Is as natural as drawing
Breath into lungs, there's more
Cars and SUVs broken into
By unknown parties than not, more
Fenced-off pieces of land and
Liquor stores than there are
Community centres and decent
Food shops, the homeless sleep
Against boarded-up buildings
Empty inside as the price of
Housing continues to soar past the clouds,
Drugs and black market guns
Are always available, have been available,
Five decades of strung-out
Black bodies and Black bodies shot
From petty disputes write that history,
Where the criminal image, the thug agenda is praised,
Where I fear the enemy & the enemy is my own—

Believe me, I didn't design this madness. I'm

Not a native, but a resident
Of my corner of East Oakland

Where poverty dominates,
But its effects are being relieved,
Mutual aid is not a theory here,
It's hitting the street running,
Seeing to a long queue of people, families in need,
Alleviating hunger, thirst, human health,
Mutual aid for the block
Takes several forms:
Black Cultural Zone,
Occur,
East Oakland Collective,
Homies Empowerment,
POOR Magazine,
These days, the working class
Around here are supporting themselves,
Since the city won't—

Downtown City Hall
Sees my place of residence
As a blemish on the east side
In need of change,
Just remove
The poor
From homes,
Rename the block,
Welcome richer
Residents in—

Like I said, I didn't design this madness.
But as long as I'm here, from my little house of six years,
I'll document it. I'm

Not a native, but a resident
Of my corner of the changing Bay Area,

Eastmont, Oakland, California, U.S.A.

Where I'm from.

Young African Man

by Evans Mwendwa Mutie

Young African man arise,
Don't sleep a little more, they'll say you're lazy
Wake up earlier, stretch a little
Yawn, I mean yawn to that stretch
Don't just stand there, look like an African
A young African man

African man arise, it's time to breakfast
It's time you collected some cassavas
Ooh! And the roots, those roots that help you work magic in bed
And some black tea, black tea and arrow roots taste like greatness
Don't forget your momma's favorite words
An empty stomach leads to an empty head

African man rise, it's time to dress up,
Pick that tie you love and a very heavy coat
Ooh! You don't like coats, then wear that Ankara
Put on some dashiki patterns, get yourself looking great
Step out like the world depends on you
Don't forget to comb those bushy beards
Maybe trim them a little
Something important your momma loves, wear that smile: she says it will
Bring you a wife soon

African man rise, it's time to go to work
What is your favorite ride?
Is it the matatu? I mean, the loud African matatu with chicken and goats
and sugarcane and rhumba?
Is it your favorite bicycle? The bicycle your father took from your
Grandfather who took it from the white man?
Is it on foot? Do you like to trudge through the dusty streets so that you
Can see your shoe shiner?

Maybe you want to see the latest newspaper

African man rise, it's time to be of service
Do you work at the cafeteria, do you work at the construction site
Are you a bouncer at the clubhouse, are you her favorite waiter *winks
African man you need a job, push those carts, play those cards
You need to do something,
You're tired, get some ice cold Coca-Cola soda
The office is getting monotonous, do small talks, do a little chatter with
Your fellow African men

African man you're tired, you've done it, you've earned it
Let them be Judges, but your Acts don't deserve Lamentations
You're a hero, you saved the day
African man go rest, take that radio, tune to your choice
Take your favorite instrument, is it the guitar?
Is it the Kayamba? Play some music

African man you love something... is it football
Is it the taste of a beer? Does it make you smile
Is it a hangout with friends?
African man rise I repeat, African man rise,
It's morning again

Morning Alarm

by Dee Allen.

It's morning again

And the first
Sound I hear
Rousing me from dreamless rest
Pulling me back into consciousness
Comes live and direct
From nature
From sky
From long, pointy black beak
Swift as the crow will fly—

Short, sharp repetitions of caws,
Calling the sleeping world to awaken.

Sounds from a black bird's throat,
More effective than
The round, battery-powered
Clock on the shelf—

Morning alarm
From Brother Crow
Stirs my limbs into rather sluggish movements,
Enables my body to rise
From the mattress on the cold brick floor,
Take six steps to the lavatory in half-light,
Flick of the light-switch and my ritual begins
From towel rack to wash cloth
To soap bar to hot shower
To sink to mirror
To can of Barbasol cream to razor—

Afterwards, I look
Forward to
My favourite
Part of this new day:

Meatless breakfast.

Hash brown patties,
Seitan bacon strips,
Bowl of applesauce,
Hot cup of peppermint tea

And cherry-coloured
Liquid vitamin
B-12 drops on my tongue,
Vegan's best friend.

Savouring it all
Like a soul kiss
From a fine sister.

Topping off the routine:

Discussing the crow's call
During the blue hour
With my pen

Through adding the next poem to my notebook.

[For The Unrated Poet from Kenya.]
[In response to the poem "Young African Man" by The Unrated Poet.]

Afraid

by Evans Mwendwa Mutie

With my pen I'm not Afraid
I'm not afraid of dying from the so-called pandemic
I'm afraid of never seeing the kids of my kids happy
I'm afraid of what everything looks like
I'm Afraid

I'm afraid of waking up each day to live in this dump site again
I'm afraid of seeing my peers develop breathing complications each day
I'm afraid that our suffering comes because trash is carried from their rich
Homes to the sides of ours
I'm afraid that they don't even think we get children here

I'm afraid
I'm afraid of the poisonous politics they dump in our midst
I'm afraid of how they pour their malicious propaganda to see my folks
Bleed for their sake
I'm afraid of the air that we breathe, the food we eat, the water... I mean
Everything
I'm Afraid

I'm afraid that the food we eat, the mandazi, they're cooked by the
Roadside
Dust and fumes from your big slick cars covers our food
I'm afraid of tomorrow
I'm afraid that I'll wake up and have to starve myself for a day so that I eat
The next day
I'm Afraid of everything

I wake up each day and the stories I hear don't add a smile to my face
Each day the story is the same, no services in hospitals, no water in the
Place, no nothing
I'm Afraid
I can't walk my streets without a heart throb, it's dark here, painful there,

It's dusty here, dirty there, I can't clean the town
I'm afraid that my people are not considered as people who need help
but Strongholds for political folks
I'm afraid that every day I'll wake up with the same story
No jobs but prisons are being added each day
That's why the bullet has become the order of the day
Sirens here and there, is it the ambulance?... ziii ni masanse wamebamba
Mrazi fulani
I'm Afraid (no, it's the police who'll arrested one of our boys)

I can't sit and watch all these without at least being afraid of my situation
I can't watch my folks rob my folks
I can't watch my brothers smoke for a living though they're asthmatic
I can't watch the world go round
My momma can't get herself a pound
In her pocket
I'm Afraid

I'm not afraid that my friends will get in car accidents but am afraid that
The roads are too favourable for accidents
I'm Afraid that my children will have to choose between two wrongs
I mean why the choice between two bad people
You know Rao* na Root oh** God, why these choices

*Rao, means Raila Odinga, a Kenyan political demagogue.
**Root oh, street name for William Ruto another political figure

IX. Halima & Caren

Giving Honor to the Gods

by Halima Olufemi

They stayed at 461 Roosevelt Circle in Presidential Hills. My Grandmother and Great-grandmother never left each other's side.

Fannie Mae was my Great Grandmother's name but we called her Bigmama. Her husband had been dead for years. She never remarried, never dated, and rarely traveled outside the house. He drove trucks for a living and built a home on about an acre of land. I think he was an older man and that she was only 15 when they got married.

She raised her family with a 3rd-grade education, survived off instinct and made a decent living. There was no time for leisure. Fannie Mae had one sibling we called Aunt Lillie and their mother was Mama Heggs. She and her sister raised themselves and both of them preceded Bigmama in death.

Being an adult the majority of her life, she experienced a lot of pain beginning with the loss of her first child. Later, she would almost die being shot 9 times—forced to live with one bullet lodged beside her spine.

When my sister and I were little, Fannie Mae drove a big blue Cadillac, wore big church hats, and white gloves to usher in the saints. Always a mother, prim and proper, she wanted us to be the same. In her own way, she protected us from the world that shaped her insanity, considered the "mean" one, I now realize she loved us fiercely.

Looking back, it is also apparent she probably suffered from depression or PTSD. She carried her anger like a gun. It was a source of protection as long as you weren't standing in front of it. Her perpetual sadness was a cry for help, but God and prayer were her only therapists. Bigmama's hugs were genuine because they were rare. She ruled with a switch or belt and was not very forgiving because life had shown her the effectiveness of cruelty.

By the time I was about 10, Fannie Mae had become a recluse rarely leaving the house; maybe walked around the block but nothing else. I can only imagine how lonely she felt sitting in her red chair with no one to turn to but God and her daughter.

Elzadia...

Our Grandmother JoJo was something else. She owned a bait shop that yielded little profit, but helped us learn how to barter. I didn't see it then, but it taught us the value of community and the importance of a dollar.

JoJo would host parties where they dyed bread green and red for the holidays and sometimes drank Kosher wine. She and her daughters would decorate buildings and step out to parties in Black sequin dresses and high heels. They let us help where we could and sip Champale when it was time for bed. Eventually, she stopped because her spiritual journey overshadowed everything else, and like most Black people looking for answers, she ran to the church.

JoJo was raised in Louisiana and originally practiced Catholicism, but her daughter, my mother, was excommunicated for having children with no husband. We flirted with Yaweh Ben Yahweh, but found out he was a crook, and finally "converted to Hebrew" instead. Like many religions, it was strict, with most of the restrictions being tossed at the feet of women.

We could only wear dresses that covered our knees, because we wouldn't want to tempt some man into looking and we couldn't wear pants and we couldn't wear our arms out and we couldn't wear make-up and we couldn't cut our hair and our heads had to be covered and we couldn't ask questions and we had to say yes sir and yes mam or we were considered bad children and the women in the church had to serve the men no questions asked and we couldn't watch TV on Saturday because that was a holy day and we needed to rest and we couldn't eat scavengers of the sea or animals whose hooves were split and we couldn't celebrate Christmas or Easter and did I mention this was when we were still attending St. Mary's School for Catholics...

Imagine... the innocent cruelty of children.

I thought then, with all the restrictions, I'm really not all that interested in heaven though I don't want to go to hell...

And it caused me great anxiety... internal agony.. .because it seemed so cruel to let someone burn in hell for eternity because of the food they eat or the clothes they wear or that they watched TV on the day you were supposed to rest...or that they would hang a man on the cross, pierce him in the side, beat him to death with a cat of nine tails, send him to hell and back to prove he loves you...

And that I watch people being punished who try to follow every tenant and every rule, practice their faith or religion while still living in abject poverty and despair while also watching those who subscribe to none of it live with no worries and thinking we have no idea what really goes on after death and those that are most sure are still guessing and how can a person's faith be deemed the right one when it's all just opinion and strong preference... and am I gone get in trouble for thinking this because he knows our thoughts and we shouldn't question him... and I don't want him to strike me down or go through nothing else or learn anymore hard lessons or be punished for thinking or doing something wrong

... this shit sounds like slavery...

We are bound to church en masse with bloodsoaked crackers that teach us to suffer and wait patiently on the return of a savior to save us from the suffering he reportedly already saved us from, while we beg for forgiveness and blame ourselves for him leaving... trauma wrapped in religion unequipped to aid in the emotional healing of Black people who consistently go through unfettered shit that includes being made to feel like we deserve it...

I dreamed of my Grandmothers the other day, they said: "forgive yourself for believing it."

Giving Honor to the Gods...

Who Are You

by Caren Jepkogei

I'm the best version of me
One who settling for nothing but the best
Defines me
No matter how bad the western winds can blow my fortunes
Just like dust I rise to light up my path
I illuminate my future

I'm the umbrella to those around me
Covering my family and close friends from the hot scorching life
Sealing holes that make rain water to drizzle on our path and peace
Holding our mantle up high is what my day looks like

I'm the shiny star in the sky
The one who shines on the life of the less fortunate
The one who lights up the life of its own people
The pretty soul who leads the rest to achieve their dreams and goals

I'm the sunrise and the sunset
Who wakes up at dawn to go get it
The one who helps mama light the fire and fetch firewood
To my people I've wiped and dried their tears
I've made the scorching sun set in their lives and replaced it with hope

I'm the broken pot at times
When lightning and thunderstorm strike my life
Drawing the energy from my knees and making me weary
I've seen days ending as soon as they begin
I've always emerged stronger

88

I'm the poet
The one whose lines drip to flowing stanza
The one who loves her work and would water your life with words
The one who gets to your heart by her words
I'm Caren
The girl who will explain her twenty-five years in words

I am a Black Woman

by Halima Olufemi

I am that voice you don't want to hear instead of that thing you don't
want to hear

A Black Woman

I am that thing you don't want to hear.
I am that beautiful reflection you see in the mirror pointing out
imperfections holding pride in one hand and doubt in the other, vying
to see who will win.

I am the construct of a past that raped confidence from my mind and
hid it between my legs so that sex would never be confused with intimacy
again.

I am brutal honesty,

wrapped in delicate skin releasing my emotions with handsome tears for
myself and all who need them. I shed the blood of dead children and
run fragile egos to caucasians for coddling wielding machetes and light-
ning as I walk. My rage needs protection not guilt trips and pillow talk.

I am your mother,

who knows you like she knows herself because she took the shots that
gave you life and died nine times to birth you. Her understanding has no
boundaries in a world that keeps us laboring to love you.

90

I am your sister,

nurtured from the same pain, seeking attention the same way, loving you with a hate that could only be related. I will get in your face, "slap-box" your soul away, then wrestle to the ground until grandmama say, "Y'all stop all that tussling gal, gone somewhere else and play"—be mad for 10 minutes then race you down the street to play dodgeball or hide-and-go seek.

I am your daughter,

you should want to protect me. Make me believe that make-believe is real, slay dragons, ignore temper tantrums and love me unconditionally with understanding and honest compassion—not disdain and gaslighting tactics.

I am your queen,

I am NOT a science project. Your ribs have nothing to do with who does the dishes, and kitchens don't care who cook in 'em and a diaper with shit in it simply needs changing and our hands work the same.

I am herbs
I am medicine
I am hard because that day soft was taken

I am the undercurrent of blue that you see in a full moon
I am incense unfurling to the sounds of Badu

I am sunshine
I am sunrays
I am waves crashing in the sea
I am doves crying to be seen

I am hurricane season exposing your treachery
I am Shug Avery running to save Ms. Celie

I am the reason Jesus wept
I am life after death
I am both heaven and hell

I am eternally blessed

I am mad at the world for their treatment of Black Women

I am tired of apologizing for owning my freedom

I am pissed that society celebrates the cruelty of misogyny and condemns
Black Women simply for resisting.

Demons,

You have no power over me
I hold thunder with my teeth
And ride tsunamis through the streets
Guiding dead bodies to come see me

I am a God
None can enter but through me
I move the world with my mind while eating vegetables and sipping
green tea

I am distant galaxies
I am dual realities

"*Yes your majesty*"
is the only thing you should say to me

I am audacity
I am sacrifice
I am everything you need

Except lily white

I am not your cotton, my life is not for sale
So keep your self-hatred and fragility over there with them

I said no,
I am not your slave

Either stand with me or get out of my way.

See, I have too much power to stay behind a desk
Or pray for some man's last name

I have my own.

Woman

by Caren Jepkogei

Either stand with me or get out of my way
For I am not just an ordinary woman
I am a virtuous strong woman

Bold enough to tear apart the demons that stand in my way
They have tormented my future and strangled my destiny
They have stood on my way up the ladder
They still have enough courage to see me fail

See
I wake up every day to fight my way up
I still gather the energy to take me through
Brighten the light for those with dim ones
I have spoken at the table of the world to fight for the woman
I still nurse emotional and mental wounds for the days I never won
I still oil my wounds with the never-giving-up spirit,
for I am a noble Woman

A woman who is stronger than her fears
A soul that strives for perfection in all shades of dull days
An unending definition of true love at heart
A idol that represents humanity when the world turns its back on us
A very broad shoulder to house those whose lives were swept away by the
Storms of life

I strive to win fights
In the midst of a society where the woman is no different than a child
In my mind as I try to figure out how I'll fight them with my mind
In my heart lives humanity
Lives a portion for winning

For I am a go-getter
Definition of nobility
Shiny star
The sunflower

The world has treated me like a glass
Fragile enough but not good enough for my strengths
Living in the hands and lying on the floor of mercies
Yes I am a queen
A precious soul
Daddy's favorite
A jewel
The princess
Grown-up Cinderella
But the world will never treat me as such
I will broaden its fingers to grab me
Neither will it ease for my pending bills

I walk in the streets today
Not a happy woman but a contented one
I still fight for my place
But at least not with my past
Giving up is not part of me
So either stand me for the woman or
Allow me to stand for her

X. Zakiyyah & John

You Never Said Goodbye

by John Otiso Bundi

It begins and never ends
I may cry this whole night
I may even cry for the rest of my life
But, I can't as I lost my right
To even break down in tears

I feel hurt when I realize
I can no longer see you with my eyes,
I can no longer touch you with my hands
But I will feel you in my heart forever

You never said "goodbye"
You promised to never leave me
You never said "I'm leaving"
Instead, you proved with your actions

A million times I needed you
If love alone could have saved you
I would have never lost you
A million times I loved you

I hate having to say goodbye,
To a friend I know I won't get
To see again in my life
Anyways goodbye and I miss u

Those Yesteryears

by Zakiyyah G. E. Capehart

anyways goodbye and I miss u
the years have been long
much too long to remember
the hurtful times encountered
in our relationship

but i do remember
the beautiful times we shared
those yesteryears were magical
and in this moment
i want to embrace our life
together again

knowing it is impossible
i cling to those memories
and mourn losing you
in physicality
albeit we will spiritually
be together eternally

as a child i did not understand
your unrelenting outspokenness
protesting so me and my siblings
could attend better schools

i wanted my mother at home safe
not out in the community
fighting for school rights

cause I heard the unkind words
and saw the hatred in the eyes
of white people that wanted
to keep black children
out of their schools

working tirelessly at home
with six children and holding down a job
you knew the importance of advocating
for your family and the community
instilling in us the necessity of education

your powerful gentle brilliance
continues to guide and fortify my life
it is the mirror that i hold
the blessings that unfold
the wisdom that must be told

I Remember

by Zakiyyah G. E. Capehart

the wisdom that must be told
back home in north carolina
remembering grandma and grandpa
feels like a huge hug that picks me up
spins me around and never lets me down

i can still smell the delectable aromas
emanating from the collard greens,
stringbeans, chicken and dumplings,
cornbread, and sweet potato pie
in grandma's kitchen

on those sweltering north carolina days
grandpa would gather me and my sisters
on the porch to sample grandma's
lemonade
quenching our thirst and listening to
the most imaginative creative stories
grandpa ever told

back when we caught lightening bugs
in jelly jars
took long exaggerated country walks
on dirt roads
sat barefoot under the shade
of elongated weeping willow trees
fanned dripping sweaty faces
in blistering church pews
on sunday mornings

a small rural town
where unconditional love
resided in the hearts
of the people in the community
replicating the village concept
that wrapped me in a cocoon...
swaddling
nurturing
protecting
so i could survive to tell the stories
from grandma's and grandpa's legacy

Sunrise Sunset

by Zakiyyah G. E. Capehart

from grandma's and grandpa's legacy
through my window shade
you peer in
and climb into my bedroom
i awake and find you
sprawled across my bed
caressing me with your warmth
kissing me from head to toe
fondling me playfully
i giggle feeling your radiant glow

frolicking throughout the day
your gaze intrigues me
from extraordinary places
we flirt
like long-distance lovers

as the day draws to an end
you move closer to me
gaining...
magical
miraculous
momentum
enormous growth and
spectacular intensifying hue

stonished and gaping
completely surrounded
wondering...
if i will be devoured by you
feeling your intense heat
to my very core
anticipating being engulfed

with eyes closed
awaiting our amalgamation
i wait...
wait
wait
a cooling dim shadiness
looms overhead
sensing change
in my environment
i open my eyes
and see you are gone

looking around
i can't see
any trace of you
my dream of our fusion
deferred...

indeed gone from view
but not from my memory
i will wait until tomorrow
when you appear once more

peering through my window shade
climbing into my bedroom
i will find you sprawled
across my bed
caress me with your warmth
kiss me from head to toe
fondle me playfully
and i will giggle
feeling your radiant glow

when the day is done
and evening come
surround me
grow enormous once more
but this time when you go
take me with you

XI. IMAHKÜS Njinga (Mama One Africa) & Christopher Okemwa

How Do You Say No In THUNDER?

by IMAHKÜS Njinga (Mama One Africa)

Grandmaw said git under dat bed when
THUNDER and lightnin' strike
God don't want no squawkin'
while she's talkin' loud this night,
just make sure yo stuff is right
as that Thunder louds up the night.
THUNDER without lightnin' is like fear that ain't frightenin'
Or a gift of a toy received without joy
and love without kisses, when you finally meet your missus,
or that very special someone.
Clap, Clap, Boom, Boom
THUNDER in the room
Slap, Slap, Boommadeboom
THUNDER sounds like doom
THUNDER in the pounding of my chest
When my love's been put to rest
And my world has gone asunder
THUNDER, THUNDER
BLUNDER, BLUNDER
Where did we go wrong?
THUNDER, THUNDER
The sound above the throng,
Of people pushing and people shoving
as they try to get away
From the crashing sounds of THUNDER
as it shatters my peace of day
THUNDER, THUNDER
I really wonder,
about the purpose that it serves
for it's just a lot of noise,
that really gets on my nerves
THUNDER, THUNDER

annoying and destroying my peace
THUNDER, THUNDER
That invisible, troublesome beast
Loud **THUNDER**
Terrifying **THUNDER**
Crashing **THUNDER**
Useless **THUNDER**
What is your purpose???
How Do You Say No In THUNDER?
YOU DON'T!

Covid-19 ? ? ? ? ? ? ? ? ? ? ? ? ? ? ? The Plandemic

A Lockdown Poem

by IMAHKÜS Njinga (Mama One Africa)

I WEPT
I wept for those who will live
I wept for those who will die
I wept for those who lied
I wept for those who died
I wept for the Mothers and the Fathers, the Sisters and the Bruthers
I wept for the whole world-wide

I wept for a world gone wild.
Where good sense became nonsense and people no longer had cents.
The rich will die with the poor and what once was, will be no more.
I wept for the Grandmothers and Grandfathers, the Aunts, the Uncles,
the Cousins, the Nieces, the Nephews and the friends
and the world we once knew but will never know again.
So, don't give up the fight African people of the Light;
long known for our might, endurance and insight.
We were Gods and Goddesses then and will certainly be that again.
African people rise up, let not this enemy destroy us.
With Love, Unity, Diversity and Trust as our thrust
Winning this battle is a definite must.
It's our time to rise up from the dust, reclaim what is rightfully for us;
Our African Birthright, our Freedom, our Trust, and Liberation a MUST.
Let's throw in the lake, Bill Gates and his mates, in the lake of fire and
brimstone where they can't atone,
for the misery they've thrown, at a world that now mourns.
It is now time to throw the wicked babies out with the bath water.
Our ancestors implore us to follow their orders and take back what's
rightfully ours; our Minds and our Dignity, and Love of our Families;
our Natural Resources, without remorses, our Rich
and our Fertile Lands.
Let us take Africa back from the foreign hands that stole our land, those
who do not love us nor mean us any good.

Africa will not be a graveyard for us, but will be
for those who come to molest us.
Listen to the reverberating voices on the wind, the voices we hear now
and the voices we heard then.
Rise up, Rise Up... my Africa and do not bend.
It is now time to send the enemies of Africa out of our lands.
It is time to rise up, oh great Africans, to institute our plan...
We will weep no more!

I, will weep no more!

I Will Weep No More

by Christopher Okemwa

I Will Weep No More
I will weep no more
For our stolen land
Stolen culture
Stolen artifacts
Stolen God
And the importation of a white god
For our brothers
Who died in the war
For our brothers
who were taken as slaves
For our brothers who were injected with syphilis
I will weep no more
The earth
Is already soaked enough with my tears
And the heavens are deafened
With my whining

I will weep no more
For the oppression
Meted out to our ancestors
The denial of dignity
Rights
Freedoms
And peace
I will weep no more
Because the sky drops rain
And washes my tears
And the stars in heaven
Twinkle hope and peace into my soul

I will weep no more
For the history of our people
That was deleted
For the lies told to our children
In history classes
For racial discrimination
Against our people
I will weep no more
Because the moon shines upon my night
And the sun
Bestows me with power
Hope and resilience

I will weep no more
For the killing of our beloved sons:
George Floyd
Breonna Taylor
Amadou Diallo
Ahmaud Arbery
Eric Garner
Elijah Jovan McClain
Tamir Rice
I will weep no more
Because their breaths
Keep rising
And have reached the heavens
Turning into rain, wind,
Stars, meteors, air,
Clouds, hills
Trees, soil
Rivers, oceans
Lakes, streams...

He Called Upon His Mama

by Christopher Okemwa

I remember
When his neck was pinned to the ground
The earth shook in terror
Tears stung our eyes
In agony
And bitterness

We cursed the
Stinking Knee
Hated the chokehold
We gnashed our teeth
And bit our lips
And we did not believe in the world anymore

I remember
When he uttered, "I can't breathe!"
The world closed its eyes in horror
Vengeance
Hatred
Rolled furiously around us
Like a poisonous wind
Our intestines coiled
Inside us
In shame and utter despair

We wondered
How a man can do
Such heinous act
To his own brother
Why
And for what reason

I remember
When he wriggled on the ground
He called upon his "mama"
To plead for his case
But his mama had long gone
Into the winds
She could hear
But could not answer

"I can't breathe" he mumbled
His pupils dilated and rolled in their sockets
Beneath the knee
His breathing diminished
"My nuts!"
"Some water please!"
"Shit!"
His limbs, slowly,
Fell apart
Energy escaped him
"I am through"
"I am through"
His mouth dropped
His eyelids closed
He stopped breathing
George Floyd was dead.

XII. Tessa & Lilian

The In Between

by Tessa Claire Hersh

Nothing I have ever known

I'm from the in between
I'm from the never been
born of the never was
where foggy clouds rest
on ground to look above

I cannot fathom
this question
of from
being easy
to know
there has never been an answer
to me
there is no box to check right
so I'll circle above

Mothers
I have two
one I lived inside
though she never wanted me
and yet was endlessly proud
she had loved me enough
she chose to give me more
she opened her palms and believed
I would get what she had hoped for

My mother
My mom
My momma who raised me
I lived by her side

protected I was not
but treasured I'd be
we cuddled and giggled
found spots
in the sun to stretch out our yawns and breathe in the warm I was an
answer to her prayers a yearning for more The final gift her baby of four

Both my mothers were white from body and life never known the com-
fort of a black mother
wrapping their love around me smelling their chest, holding me tight
to be home as black woman is a journey
I've been left on my own

Two fathers I'm from
biological is one
Kenyan born and raised
in DC with his brother
and daughter
I am told
he did not believe in adoption
though I have never met him in life
to him I have never really been gone

My father
My dad
My Poppadoc one
always my greatest inspiration
a doctor a healer an energy reader
he saw the gods dance within me
and knew the gifts I had brung
he is ferocious in love and ego as well
he is generous obsessed and stubborn as hell
with his work on his mind
to scientists he prayed
the heart of a romantic
he taught me to listen
to hear the whispers between
the grass and the wind
the way trees held each by choice
played games with figs and fruit and presented

all of life with a royal voice

But none of these
pathways
I call home

Brooklyn, New York
where I felt most aligned
my skin smells like cinnamon, curry, berbere, and salt
but my grandmama served me bagels and lox
on a silver platter with a grapefruit cut in half
served with a grapefruit spoon
the only spoon I was told to use
like their love it didn't fit
a belly too shallow to hold my juice the edges not smooth
serrated
to cut fruit in
manageable bites
nothing messy or loud
easy to cut yourself on a spoon the only one provided
the only one allowed

I know lakes and patient land
jumping off docks
swimming with guppies
grilling what we caught

From city and farms
cul-de-sac lands
my home I'm still searching
I am building a plan

My home is with me
the love I have built
a coven of friendships
I've threaded family from silk
with fingers of a seamstress
made careful selection
I've bled for this family
each and every one

My husband holds me
with his cinnamon skin We
push our foreheads together
merging into kin
Our curls intertwine
he was made for me
silly quick witted
stubborn challenging
and Oh So fine

My faith is belonging
though not what I was taught
I pray to a myth a lore
a figment of a knowing
a yearning I've caught
a place I am going
belonging is my practice
a leap I will take
something I hope for in faith
nothing I have ever known

Daddy Had a Dream

by Lilian Omonga

I remember
Daddy had a potential dream
So beautifully amazing
Unique and gratifying
How he yearned daily
For it to come true
Was more than willing
To gladly give his all
So as to serve his purpose
But sadly enough
It never came to be.

The charismatic ones said
A pot breaks at the doorstep
My daddy's dream
Was on the verge of flourishing
When it broke into a million
Unrecognizable, useless pieces
And left him a terribly
Heartbroken man
Unbelieving and untrusting.

Such an insightful man
Was not an innate genius
But he who always
Believed in the maxim:
Always give your best.
Exceptionally skilled
Determined and a true mentor
But his only dream was
Snatched right in his presence
He had to accept his fate
Numbness dissolved into

Excruciating pain
That hurt so deeply.
What a tremendous loss!

His zealous nature
Changed drastically
He wanted to belong
But he never did fit in
He therefore opted
To be an introvert
Enjoying his own company
A great loner for that case
Still he had to battle
Through the disbelief
Of parting with his dream.

He was denied a chance
To prove his worth
By those he highly held
Those he looked up to
And blindly believed
That they always had his back
And his best interests
In their hearts
By the very ones
He considered family
But how mistakenly wrong
He was in easily trusting
His own blood.

He was beside himself
Not knowing what to do
He had had several
Rough blows in life
But this was unacceptable
But all in all
This was fate
And he had to accept it
My daddy had a dream
That never came to be.

I Remember

by Tessa Claire Hersh

dancing in the grass
running through sprinklers
leaving the pool
only for the adult swim break
a chance to eat
a bag of Andy's hot fries
with chlorine-pruned hands

I remember
Italian icees
an entire day in the sun
biking everywhere
making grass and trees
into houses and castles

I always pretended
I was a college student
it was as old as I could make-believe

my teddy bears could talk
and I was very thoughtful
about their feelings
never wanted to leave one out

lying on my belly listening
to the conversations through the floor
lying on my back staring at the ceiling
living in the house upside down
It would feel so good to have no furniture
more room to roll around
The morning glories bloomed because I spoke to them
our dogs Misty, Chrissy and Didi

I told them everything
my father was the funniest man alive
and could make my belly ache with laughter

oldest brother a mystical creature
came home from the army with spicy Korean soups
I was desperate to impress him by eating

sister tall, graceful, cool, and truly perfect in my eyes. I copied everything
she did including the way she curled her shoe laces. I'd sit under the piano
while she played and let her music shake my breath through me. I cried
when I couldn't cream cheese my bagel as pretty as she could.

today
my father is dying
George Floyd already dead
his murderer found guilty
my hair graying so fast I can't catch it
my brother has failed me
big sister looks small
my arm sore from the vaccine
my heart aching from blood drawn by the white nurse of supremacy

the pains of disappointments linger longer than the sting of a
freshly ripped knee on gravel
sweetness comes as a respite from the overwhelm rather than a break
from the fun

I remember how good it felt to be alive
thighs aching
peddling up
the hills are so steep now
the summits so low

I pray for the sweetness of life found in June, eating fresh picked
strawberries in cut-off shorts from jeans I've outgrown.

I pray to taste the crisp air while laughing and not from drowning
joy is more than a break from the inhumane

Our hearts stare at 3 generations of Civil Rights leaders
talking into a microphone celebrating a win whose bar was far too low

We praise god for the justice he has served

but my jaw is still angry
my sternum still breaks

his knee is lifted
he's been restricted
they say we can breathe but I want to collapse

sweet strawberry warm joy
burying our bellies from laughs
gasping for air
I remember freedom from attack

My Pride

by Lilian Omonga

Strong love
I have in my heart
For a wonderful
So beautiful
So serene
So fabulous
Very noisy and chaotic
Yet calm in a special way
And I call it home sweet home.

Every morning we are assured
Of the rising sun from the east
And its setting to the west
Leaving a spectacular
Scenario worth admiring
With the light clouds
Giving way to the numerous stars
And the king of the night
The moon
To take over the quiet night.

The streets are extremely lively
With all sorts of musical genres
It's not a surprise here
If you are caught up in the dance
And get lost in the trance
With all the fanfare going on
You might really mistake it

For a showground
Still it is my home.

We love visitors
So when we stare at the streets
Do not get alarmed
Just smile and wave at us
And see the charming smiles
Display in our delighted faces
We may giggle a little
That's an assurance
That you are most welcomed.

My heart is in my home
My home is my pride
And so am in love
With the conducive environs
The indigenous trees
The exotic mammals
The hummingbirds
The carnations and oserian flowers
Are a true definition of nature
And this is my pride.

I dwell in a wonderful place
The Great Rift Valley to be precise
From afar
You can never fail to notice
The evergreen canopy
The meandering rivers
The large fresh and salty lakes
And hey, did I mention
The fertility of the place?
I call it Pride Land
My home, my pride.

XIII. Tongo & Bonface

A New Dawn

by Tongo Eisen-Martin

See this rose budding a new dawn
Like a prophet getting better with time
Broom handle made paint brush or laughter briefly fitting a psalm
Fitting song scraps into chain gang trousers writing poems for people
standing in the light

The part of the art where we almost introduce a father or the family
hurricane
blinded by a living room full of moment
I wish to see each one before my end

Imperialists marching children into a bottle with downward dialogue
With white wall faces
With a ballad decorated with animal skin
the street giving them a blanket and a cheaply made hatchet
If you look in every lung, there are burns in the shape of state emblems
The problem is that when God comes, I usually have nothing to get off of
my chest. I just sit there like a man hunted. That is one piano to replace
me. That is one knife on the way.
The Nile goes rigid.

Still I Will Remember

by Bonface Nyamweya

And there will be fire
Around our cooking stones at night
Dwuooooh! Burning and vomiting sparks of light
Oh Mother Africa! Look at me
Why is history blind to your sweat?

Before Columbus, we were in America
Upon the pathways from Guinea Africa
Whistling and chanting in mouthfuls
Our legend songs of Cleopatra and such other mantras
Then came Columbus and turned us slaves

Wipe your tears for the long way gone
Though the hand of history has been biased
To render your sons and daughters insignificant
Yet we know their contributions as magnificent
Pivoted with pain, wit, sweat, and blood

Don't cry, Mother Africa
Let me weep on your behalf
But first turn me blind
That I may not see violence reign
Upon the land of humanity again

But if you turn me blind
Still I will remember the scorching tears
Of your sons and daughters across the globe
They all cry,
"We aren't lesser beings! We are full human beings!"

So switch off first my ears
That I may not hear hatred
Rolling pain in these streets of this world
To intimidate a race as a rat in the wild
Oh mother Africa, draw near, put off my ears

But if you switch off my ears
I'll still hear the inner cry of our African ancestors
Singing aloud the alphabet
Of the African dream of Ubuntu
That mantra that we all matter and coexist as a family

We shall overcome
Wisdom is pouring and all are tapping it into their hearts
Greed and pride are strolling
Into the abyss of childishness and nothingness
Humanity is eating cheese as a family soaked in love

Ambivalent Wine

by Tongo Eisen-Martin

The pullover of love has turned costly

The guitar that failed the world

this sketch spinning in unmarked air
a horn's breastplate pierced by a roman soldier

an elder declaring, "if your childhood
didn't at times involve a call to arms
then you must fight your way out
of the slavers' pocket now"

Applause as interpreted by the professed desire to go home
a ghost whose consciousness has dwindled down to one memory, a favor-
ite time of night, and a general direction to dance towards

The useless old man is me again/White industrial entertainment/"You
kill me here; I will sing Motown in the sky. What makes a man sing about
the clothes he wants to be buried in?"

The planet has only terrible poets tonight

Death in threes... fours... fives... whatever suits these scaffolds

I have settled into my pain, Lord
Put my window down next to the bus stop shelter

a mind not slow
just ambivalent to the engineering
of most cities

ambivalent about receding political economy

My grandfather's ghost
wants nothing to do with this scene

A revolutionary's laughter that becomes a side door of the universe...
explains our take on liberation—in part—the invention of a new mother-
hood
and a new universe to host it

with giant steps she learned how to use knives in america

Red Summer state of spirits
Also, pigeon imperialism expressed through a rose period

—Pick up the gun and learn something about your mind—

What else is there to do besides stop singing?

finish letters to Viet Nam then sit still

Cue empire and a monolith of mothers carrying babies
from one side of the holding cell to the other

a mountain moved into the mass soul

Don't look for a nuanced communist manifesto

walking around the world with this fire

My mother doesn't care
About your white house refund

Your utopia meetings

It's the devil who has been
ducking her for decades
devil hiding
with puppet-presidents
turning wine into humans

and there she was... keeping pace with electricity

A crowded room singing the perfect blues

Fidel near a kind word
Nuclear ego on the chopping block
Friends in need of a martial art

an atmosphere of close calls

or the whites of soldier eyes made more communal
pigs attempting to skip history
meeting their makers wearing
shades of an acceptable minor key
and industrial wine

clenched jaw gains a reckoning

the point of creation
to keep talking about the people

Because the military industrial complex has the lower 9th on a string
we look for you there
on all paths revolutionary

We have spirits who talk to and through you

federal surveilled early-dinner and the foothills of ancestor-possession

sleeping outside your body

mulling over revolutions and revolution-impressions

Good books floating around the room, baby
we're talking about non-religious, but ridiculously spiritual people, baby
ready to tutor an imperialist's blood
ready to improve our applause

I can run to any rock

I have a mother
where there was
and there will be fire

Nourishment

by Bonface Isaboke Nyamweya

The food I want isn't ready
Because I want a whole plate
Of love of neighbour
Deep-fried in freedom and peace
Served with warm regards of optimism
Drained of cold pessimism
Added delicacies of authenticity
And chewable bones of autonomy
With a stake of communal spirit
And a glass of silence at last
Is what I need
For my tummy is empty
And my mouth has nothing
And my plate is fully depleted
While my palate is so drained and dry
I want a balanced diet of care served to all
Black and white, both need this diet of love and care, always.

PART TWO:
Nigeria to West Oakland

I. Nana & The 78th Psalmist

WhatsApp

by Nana Boateng

You've got to realize Africa was condemned to ashes by the first world.
At the time, there were only two radio stations both in Accra.
The a.m. transmissions spat a colonial babbel on short waves mixed
with pigeon that **Oborɔnyi** knew would scatter
receptively cross-continental.

*Chile, **Mepakyɛw.***
At lunchtime, his portable radio sat in the middle of the bachelor camp
as he pled the disc jockey to play her song.
 "Listen to *Request Time* in 3-5 business days," he wrote to her.
The road project had taken him from home indefinitely and provided
few opportunities if any to date other women.

I didn't know what she liked to listen to, so I let the DJ pick.
The postman insisted 3 cedis wouldn't be enough to send the postage to
Accra in time, but 10 extra cedis could get it there overnight.
In the charcoal heat, his cracked hands massaged the droplets resting on
the roof of his lip until he heard Chile sputter into frequency, "Agoooo,
Maaha, we've a special requester, Sam for Ama."

And you know, your mother was the only one I was dating at the time.
His mother never went to school, but she taught herself to read the Bible
in our language. She warned him to take the girl wherever opportunities
lied, she said let Elijah and Sarah humble your journey. The girl might
turn your luck.

Did dadda ever tell you he loved you?
"You know, Walmart and your daddy ruined my American dream."

A Lifetime Ago

by The 78th Psalmist

Walmart and your daddy ruined my American dream.
I remember how only a lifetime ago I was living a Nigerian Nightmare.
Shape-shifting from white collar jobs to round neck aprons
On Sooty suits; bakery labor was the only way to earn daily bread,
Rolling pins over dough to cater for my kneads.

Mornings I stitched the Alarm clock to my Rib cage
Let the ground discover my running feet on the bustling street,
"I must not be late to anywhere except my funeral!"

I remember...
How we cracked jokes and Knuckles over meatless meeting meals
& Gaped into cheap soups and found nothing fishy.
Cement mixed with sand mixed with iron was concrete evidence
Of how back-battering scorching suns boiled us to sweats like bad temper.

Nigeria was killing; I was dying to get out.
The autopsy came in a green leathered passport and stamped visa.
It's like democrats' votes, they say
"Giving up is for-biden"
So what if Walmart and your daddy ruined my American dream?

How Do You Read Water?

by *The 78th Psalmist*

When historians ask me to fetch my ancestors,
I serve them the ocean in a bowl.
Watch its viscous content sway, like the angst of a slave coffle,
Dangle my grip loosely & just enough to hear the water whisper:
Hold me gently, careful not to spill the truth of my becoming,
Hold me gently, my rippling is a language fighting not to drown.
Ghost stories of chattel-thirsty vessels, some as long as a sigh,
Dragging themselves to the haggard shore,
A Jonah too salty to be swallowed.
This is how we read water.

This is how we read water,
How we speak a language by being bubble-headed,
holding our breath and sinking.
For what is water, if not a prisoner?
Gas molecules bound by the despondence of chemistry.
Aren't the tides, the water's way of staging an uprising?
Like the bound people at Ebo Landing,
There are prepositions of mass suicides docked between these sentences.
A worn out friction between ocean and wood.
How do you read water?

Cottonmouth

by Nana Boateng

How do you read water? Does it come as a steamed morning dew
or divine, vaporized breath? Perhaps corroded and leached?

In Flint, they read water like a forgotten monthly subscription
or past due bill the debate collector's sent.

Redlines cross and dot eyes, a dry reminder
attorney generals and governors heave.

100,000 bottles of water per week will have you thinking
they'd irrigate the Sea of Galilee into a Dasani.

Knock one down, pass it around for 2 counts of involuntary
manslaughter on the wall. Loosened sludge is easily acquitted

with brand name gauze and UV filtration
from a modern American's bloodstream.

There's no fixer for salt, limestone, or simply being Black.
It'll bacteria, a flared growth, that's what changes flavor.

They'll ask, Are you not an American?
If your water isn't a little dirty,

grizzled and smeared, this is how we read water.

In the booth of a crowded Golden Corral, I spill
my third refill of Hi-C Orange, bibbing towards
a speckled resin edge.
This is how I read it.

A wet bed, dirtied by comfort.
Sucking my thumb, a pruned, gilled alloy.
This was my water.

What is water, if not to gift relief?

II. Adeyinka & Lisa

On Her Shoulders I Stand

by *Adeyinka Ireti Aromolaran*

Her story I tell as a tale.
Yeye Moremi, with tolerance demystified and unmasked
Igbo Warriors,
Brought calm to the most curious and furious!
Peace soon soothed Ile Ife,
But her sacrifice, to some, seemed unfair.
Queen of Zauzzau reflected equality on saddles for liberation.
Her courage was a conquest for subjugation.
Our mothers are champions
Not effigies with sale tags and coupons.
I'll wail, hail, and echo their names, for they are icons.
But in her story, travail and name are trampled upon as cobs of corn.
My chant to these heroines on the honour rolls
Not cowards who dock in the hermit's hole.
Maami, Moremi, Harriet, Efusetan, Hazel Olumfunmilayo,
Amina, Aimiuwu, Emotan!
XX no boundaries.
They moved beyond borders
Going against the tides
Aje... what you're called for standing by your own.
True, because you truly won't stare till yours, like a shaft, is blown!
Maami, the firm tripod stand that sits and not let its content pour or sour
I sit and sleep on your beaded waist,
Fastened with your cotton sash and snore.
Aje... because when I call,
You heed lest I fall.
The only loose ends I see are the twines, raffia, broken iron garlands that
Held us captives...
Let it be—We contend and not pretend!

Let Us Not Pretend

by Lisa D. Gray

Let it be—
we contend and not pretend that we do not recall babies
marching for freedom down streets built on the backs of nameless
souls—their dusky hues rendering them invisible for eternities.

Let us not pretend that just last year,
last month,
last week,
yesterday
blue monsters did not smother another mother's hope.

She reaches for starlight sitting on the back porch, and her fingers pluck
memories from sky as sirens wail a song of death. The hole in her heart
now grown round enough for her to slip into its dark depths as she sits
smoking a Newport,

a
tear
tickling
her
nose.
She wants him back.
Her Sonshine
...but
no marches, no juries, no prayers will resurrect his precious body,
a threat.

So she sits on the back porch remembering.

My Dirge, My Kiln

by Adeyinka Ireti Aromolaran

She sits on the back porch remembering
Events as the images unfold
Like a rolled strip of horror films
Ready to be washed in the dark room
To tell a gothic story.

Going down memory lane...
I remember... that She is me.

He was clothed in a black and white striped shirt.
All I perceived was sweat
All I saw was filth
All I felt was dirt
With an accent he yelled,
Commanded to be held.
My little, brittle, fragile fingers
Went through his hair and beard.
I remember...
That very act and scene of the play,
Its performance in its entity
Was a tragedy accompanied with dirge,
My dirge, but no one was there to listen
To my lament,
To cut the scene, end the "play"
Or change the script, talk less of the script.
If there was a listening ear, who would it hear?
The truth, the truth, was a nightmare of fear
Fear, fear, daring fear that stifled a word!
Gagging the mouth with the threat of sword!
Like an oath forced on a meal of life crab
For confession unheard, the way out of his ominous stab.

I remember...
The family get-together
Adults swaying left to right to the tune
Of highlife music back in the '80s
Raising a toast to each other.
Maami saying, "sit on his lap, he is your uncle."
To her, he was so trusted like the Oracle
But to me,
His lineage calls were for his pleasure and spectacle,
Ere tete
I'd rather take solace with my pet than for a tête-à-tête.
I remember calling...
"Maami!"
"Shhh! Let's talk later."
She filled my mouth with chunks of batter.
As the get-together rolled in frolicking Bata
While I in forced silence swallowed my words
And just listened to the melody, their chords.

But for many haunting years I remember
Plagued by what I choose to do with it,
Shall I be downcast and pitied?
Or wield a weapon to fight against the tide of torturous memories
Of teen years—regarded by many now as a fiction on fairies.

But I refuse to wallow in such turbulence.
These thoughts built a mind kiln....
A kiln to bake all the wedged, kneaded, moulded.
Experiences sieved into fine clay,
Thrown on a wheel to create a masterpiece.

I emerge an earthenware glazed with timeless memories
Filled with the challenging times of teen years.
I have come of age and I refuse to be broken or caged
With memories of that phase.
I stand as a terracotta brick wall
Fortified by horrid days of teeming years
I have made me a warrior shield
To win my own battles, for I'll not yield.

I choose to challenge the life's experience(s)
And rise as an overcomer
For it's time to celebrate who I have become
Against all odds,
I AM TERRACOTTA.

Dear Mom

by Lisa D. Gray

Missing you today.
Time stopped when you had to leave.
So hard to let you.
Thinking of your smile,
memory washes away
and summer comes again.
I still cry at night
and while shopping on weekends
for groceries and weed.

160

III. Duana & Jeremiah

Reverie in Reverse, Placebo Medicine

by Duana Fullwiley

In a forward rock, his body spoke
eyes tunneling a passageway

A giddy glee,
sensate plea,
punctuated by point of interrogation:
Why can't I just take his pain?

Episodically ill,
this Senegalese questioner,
born with capricious blood,
visited a child's sickbed

Chronic with history

His own cells had moods,
roiling bad days

Survival required art

He sketched the disease a place in him, drew her a body and mind,
eked out a life for her
in relief
to dance together

Conjoined
congenitally

His ached attention
soothed her upsets,
unplugged bad dreams,
triaged traumas,

boiled plant medicine
to reverse
systems of noxious neglect

Appeasement,
always a gamble

Uncertainty, the common law of love
and science

Darling, I'm here for you
'Til death do us part,

No.
Even then, it's you and me.

His *maladie*[1]
heart melody
primary relationship

invited in,
as kin,
all with shared sickle blood[2]

The pebble bony child,
skin thin,
yellowing eyes,
wadded in sheets,

torqued and tied,
writhed,
reached out to him

Again
the questioner rocked forward,
arched in a healing bond,
straddling the sonic chasm of the metronome,

---

1   "Maladie," or illness, in French is gendered feminine.
2   In Wolof "bokk deret" literally means to share blood and is an idiomatic expres-
sion to mean one's "relative," or "family member."

his own pulse vibration,
signaling
an arrival

The boy, too stunned to move,
cells jammed in veins,
mourned the fatality of his once fetal blood,
ossifying

Tears tearing through stillness,
senses hijacked by hurt

Once more,
the curious one rocked forward,
toward the small person,
unfurling a telepathic undulation

Code of pathos unspooled
Why can't I just take his pain?

Unthinkable?

A lack of moral imagination
Requires rescue of principled instructions

1: Update transfusion technology from intravenous to *intrabeing*

Trust.

2: Sense heartbeat, pressure, temperature

Then suture.

3: Infuse the other with the transient ease

of your own mortal vitality
in a slow stream

Finally, chelate their crises of solitary suffering

Can't we share our surplus health?

This embodied care of placebo medicine,
perhaps, perhaps,
reigns just below the dermal-blood barrier,
monetarily *free*

Yet it may cost us

Our precious
coined rationality

Ọmọtoyosi Ọpẹyẹmí

by Durotinu Jeremiah

Coined rationality,
I hope this is rationale,
The year 92,
To everyone it holds different meaning
To the Manchester United team,
It speaks of a group of players,
That formed the core of their most successful years.
I'm not a fan though
For my own team
The year 92
Saw the introduction of a future legend to the club.
For me as an individual,
92 was a year of drastic change
A year of loss
Loss of what might have been
A loss of hope
Loss of a birthday mate
Loss of a playmate
Loss of memories that could have been made
Loss of siblingship
The loss of who could have become a confidant
The year 92
A year of changed status,
Which ushered in a new responsibility,
Daily I ask,
What could have been?
The tears that drop
When in solitude thinking of you,
Carry the emotions,
I never got to share with you
If you were still here.
A year together wasn't enough

A year,
The gap between our ages,
Daily I hope for more,
No memory to talk about you
Save a singular picture.
You live continually in me,
The sister,
I never knew, yet I met, loved.
I love you through
The two wonderful sisters
Who came after,
I love you through
Your many namesakes around me
I love you through our parents,
They remain the bond that ties us forever.

Sand Lines

by Duana Fullwiley

We build castles on sands,
while the grit of our future dissolves

The powdered earth now streaming between fingers,
scattered nascent by breeze

The bliss of having lost our way,
we meander through granules and minutia

Reminders of our smallness,
grace
remembrance of our source

The metric tons of ocean that polish each potential
speck of silica,
silt white,
call our pulses by other names

Crest the wave of calm in veins,
join the high tide of belonging

Surrender to the pull of moon blood,
in the swell of the sea foam body

That form we share stretched over deserts
beyond the depths of the zaffre blue bottom

There we fuse,
in the clarity of dream
between life,
fire and bone colored cloud

Can I Go Back?

by Durotinu Jeremiah

Can I go back?
The days when relationships meant a lot
The days when friendships
Weren't based on material help
Rather mutual connections of pains and pleasure
Pleasure of victories won
Pains of battles lost.

The building of a fraternity that lasts long
The days of genuine relationships
When we were not moved by clicks on social media
The clout chasing and the likes
Popularity contests
Weren't the order of the day.

When we rolled tyres with sticks
Meeting after school
Our uniforms told their stories
Dirtied and stained
Even till now
When talking about then
It brings back memories
It gladdens the heart truly.

Friendship is a bond.

We all grew up cherishing each other
Knowing that our words won't be used against us
Your secrets didn't become tales for comic relief.

Wish I could go back
To experience true friendships.

IV. Godfrey & Amos

For She Who Already Knows She Knows

by Amos White

Women like you are walking scriptures.
Written in every way
the intelligence of design crosses every man's heart

for women like you walk in scriptures.

Verses unfolded beneath
behind and under—
his shadow soul, his home, his self

for women like you are walking sculptures.

Alabaster stammers and cowers
to Ebony
Ivory, too, sheds its luster
before your Nubian hues.

Before Your Nubian Hues

by Godfrey-Elvis Odianose

Before his dreams lived
Before your ivory sheds its luster
Before his Prophecy was fulfilled
I saw him die that day.

I remember it was a cool evening,
with orange sunsets painted in the sky getting darker.
Young kids playing and running around
untiled streets gutter oozing out
the smell of a dead fish.

People passing by hurriedly,
as if ascending and descending the underdeveloped street
fear hanging atop their shoulders.

Everyone was eager to find shelter before dark
lest they could be another victim.
But the kids were more interested in rolling out
motorbike tyres while dawning wild smiles on their faces.

I remember,
he walked past me while I stared at the sky
its amazing picture painted out with the strokes of God's hands.

He was bathed in blood.
His clothes were ripped off his neck,
His eyes whispered amazing grace.
His mouth drooling for help,
His body too weak to kick in energy to run for safety.

I was astounded and gripped with fear,
as I saw men in black uniforms,
badges of brutality on their shoulders.
Wearing berets of intimidation armed with guns of death.

The men in Black, walked towards him.
They made life a living hell for him,
I must confess... Hell would have been safer for him.
I heard one of the men in Black say, "We go kill you and nothing dem go
fit do" another said, "After we don kill you, we go carry your car go" and
lastly another said,
"Young people of nowadays, where dem dey see this money sef."

These were men meant to protect the society,
men who wore black so they could be white.
Instead, they became the devil himself.
Inflicting pain on the flag of green and white.

I saw them beat him to death.
Here, extra judicial killings have become the norm.
No one can raise their hands up in objections.
Everyone shuts up the truth in their bones
so they can have a slim chance of breathing tomorrow.

I saw his face after he was left for dead,
the hope on his face was blind.
It's sad, those kids rolling out motorbike tyres
will be dead someday for owning cars.

Now, the men in Black wear blue.
A colour meant for the sky, is now a symbol of brutality here.
Here is no safe.
Here, we have lived in such darkness that it takes blindness to cure us.
Here is Nigeria.

Here Is Nigeria

by Amos White

Here is Nigeria.

I remember the color blue in more than the meaning of the sky
when our hearts filled with the air, we never felt the thought of not
having it—
of butterfly wings and societal hurricanes in confluence

dinner bowls steamed with stew, cooling grandpa's temper
when mouths cool our spoons the laughter will spill into the room
with backyard dreams and recountings of pirates falling from the roof of
the shed

Here is Nigeria.

I remember the song sound rising from dad, rising for you like Om
when our souls brimmed, full bellies glowed and only our smiles gave us
away
between toes tapping and head bobbing in a rapper's delight

the rocks hopped the lake like a frog across a pot of boiling water
when your arm split the air and my forehead ran red after the lightning
broke
on peels and groans

Here in Nigeria

I remember—
I remember
I remember

178

Here, Nigeria

dances in my throat or my mind's eye every time grandpa's story runs
Anansi would win
when all that is or can be, is all that there was or ever shall be,
his voice reminds me—his voice reminds me—

Still I Call It Home

by Godfrey-Elvis Odianose

Tell me, have you ever lay next to someone
tried to breathe like them almost dead?
Well I have, because I come from a bloodline
of bleeding youth, asking for daily bread when they own the bakery.

I have strived and thrived to build an identity for myself.
Yet my ID still echoes green, stained with blood
white designed by curses, with tears making it a flag.

Still, I call it home.

I was ten years young, when I witnessed pressure
talk down to my older brother, like I didn't look up to him.
Like, he wasn't a king always in his big pants trouser
with a smile that speaks about war ending and peace rising from the
ashes.

I can recall my heart became a clenched fist,
bearing knuckles aimed towards the wall asking punching questions.
I remember vividly that day, the journey back home was a solemn one.
Mother threw her smile at the back seat and her joy traveled somewhere
distant.
Siblings forgot what happiness is
while they looked through the window of despair.

Few days later, I saw him in a morgue.
His face became an abandoned wedding on a Saturday.
And I was an awaited item 7 sitting in the front seat.

Not knowing what to do at that moment so I mimicked his feigned
smile,
I figured that if we have the same face that day
then maybe he will remember that I am his brother
waiting for him to rise on the third day.

Clean, dirty?
This question doesn't have anything to do with what happened.
The answer is we are being killed by the police
so often that I'm starting to believe that young
Nigerian bodies make good fertilizer.

Still, I call it home.

My story is a birthmark that I have learned to wear proudly.
I stand as one but I breathe ten thousand stories.
I have carried many storms with me.
I have swept myself ashore.
I have been the tide and lighthouse.
Becoming me did not come easy.

I have let my mistakes play.
Forgive me, I have doubted God in three languages.
I have stripped my flesh to reveal broken
angels pressed onto my soul.

I am my night and my sunshine.
In darkness, I have seen the devil begging me to end it all.
I have stitched myself slowly, gone to war and won myself back.
I have become too right for the left, and too left for the right.
Although my smile keeps getting arrested for no reason

Still, I'll call myself home.

V. Ifeanyichukwu & Kevin

Origin

by *Kevin Dublin*

Intoxicate minds of all who lip them
says my cousin. Or was it my brother?
Or was it another or anyone at all?
I come from a place where memory
slips as easily as fingers across a silk
dreadlock headwrap. I come from loblolly pines
lining the highway, from the taste of smoke
from a backyard barbecue, even when you
don't eat meat. I come from train whistles
and routine rumbles shaking humid
bedroom between evening junebug songs
and a radio tuned to Foxy 107/104.
Grey fox, fox squirrel, flying squirrel,
white tail deer that call this land home.
Land green with grasses, with cotton
and tobacco fields ancestors would work,
and golden mud they would walk across
as much as they would swim in—the Neuse—
a river that the Neusiok people once tended—
the Neuse—a river my father learned to swim in
in his youth as much as what he barely escaped—
the Neuse—now polluted with decades of hog waste:
thousands of nitrogen sick fish sunbathe along shores.
I come from the earth, like seedling's radicle work
to claim March sun and say this is my light.
Have you ever seen a yellow daffodil open up?
I come from exodus and bloom, from searching
for the difference between to heal and to cure.

From a forty-year-old pregnant after another
miscarraiage, from neurodivergence and beginnings
anew. From the kuh kuhn kuh kuhn kuhnck
of skateboard wheels over sidewalk cracks
on Wilmington nights and afternoons—
head bobbing between headlights, behind shrubs.
I come from the Mars dust toned gleam
of a street drummer's skin in the sun,
from the pattern in a mother's skirt
as she leads her toddler to dance to the beat,
on Market St. in San Francisco from the sun
greeting somewhere behind fog and Bay
Bridge expanse. I come from a nod
to every Black man I pass from Bryant & Beale
in San Francisco to Telegraph Ave & 18th St
at Cafe Van Kleef in Oakland, from a year of pandemic
growth untwisted to locs fit together ten years
which begin with Ms. Angie, Oakland's finest
loctician and end in hands that first braided in Senegal.
I come from an oh'three extending beyond sixty seconds
at the end of a digital clock when the police pull me over,
from two officers's hands over holster as a murder of crows
scatter from lampposts like a dark dandelion blown
by exhale and summer wish with a djinn. I come from a place
where making a living means more than fighting for rights
and it was designed to be that way, like a cypress tree
with roots deep in a dark swamp. It's hard to resist
when you must prioritize survival. I come from laughter
and long embraces from aunties, from the rustle
of a few dollars from a suit pocket into a collection plate
as "You Brought Me from a Mighty Long Way"
tenderly escapes the mouths of the alto section of choir,
from, *look to your neighbor and say, 'neighbor!'*
I said that I want you to say 'neighbor!'
'He brought me from a mighty long way.'

Reassurance

by Ifeanyichukwu Onwughalu

He brought me from a mighty long way
Now I journey back west to east
From a surgery aborted midway into puberty
That her lungs may heal and lift her reality.

Will I unbundle my thoughts as we speed along
As the antelope leaps high away from its pursuer?
Or should I reminisce my worries in this pilgrimage of assurance
Before we go in for the knife?

In the shadow of frenzied thoughts
I ask
Will it go well?
In the midst of these doubts and faiths
Laced like twins in present scenario
I pique:
Will she live?

Half a decade has been served:
Flurry of escapades deserving
Voluminous tales.
We all got drunk in passion of help,
The size that filled a bank.

Now lighting the lamp
To that long pathway to surgery room—
Not of pain but of life I see,
Not of tears but of hope it'd be
That her limbs will fly again

That this heart can breathe aloud
And all once dead come to life.

Such that sun lies side by side with earth,
In handshake of solidarity that heaves a sigh;
Such that surgeons dance with nurses,
In tributary of success in crescendo of applause.
And when wheeled out of rebirth to begin anew
Glowing shall it be
The colours of her new life.

The Colors of Her New Life

by Kevin Dublin

for Ifeanyichukwu Onwughalu

Amen, we have bodies
that know what it means
to feel seasons change

Thursday's tire tracks
grooved into sand
as night disintegrates

into dawn

morning short
in stretched hammock
hungry for more hours

the day is starving

I come out of silence
pushed only by tangerine calls
of California scrub jay

in Pioneertown

America's promise: ice tossed
between two Joshua trees
their root systems

thirst and wait

The golden-crowned sparrow
glides between these trees twice
settles on the ground beneath them

as I write

the air warms with ancestors
a plump chuckwalla basks in
their light on a rock

as I write

I'm not a body
I have a body
carried on the breeze

as I write

my ancestors and yours
on the skin. I thank them
like wild poppies bloom

as I write

I know a cousin is covering me now
as sure as I am my mother was
in last night's moonlight

as I write

a man I have never met toasts
my sideburns, and I turn my cheek
towards trunk of the tree

as I write

I remember a laugh
with a woman from Ghana
branches greet spider's web in the wind

as I write

phantom as she pricks me—
my arm: an olive branch
to a virus

as I write

a woman your close kin
who loves you deeply
glimmers in the heat haze

as I write

the fear of death
is only another worry
of exile

as I write

someone brings first sweat to my scalp
and cools me down, balmy allowance
like the chuckwalla

as I write

the truth: people living
in the street

isn't a democracy

as I write

no one dies from lack of healthcare
afros all picked out freely
with no picks

as I write

my father: a sparrow's talons

wrap around leaves of yucca plant
to hold steady & sing upwards

as I write

survival: a kind of sunrise
childhood: a faith
we outgrow

as I write

clear as the air I breathe,
curved wings of vaux's swift flock
all upturn—

as I write

forever and ever,
Asé

Notes to Gogo

by Ifeanyichukwu Onwughalu

AMEN!

SO ENDS
My prayer for Gogo
This rainy night,
Wedded by freezing breeze,
Brought fond memories of you.

I SEE YOU
In the mirror Gogo:
Even in the darkest times of the night
I see you still;
I close my eyes. I go back to
Teenageville—
It all comes clear, bold and real.

I LONG
To kiss the sweet aroma
Eavesdropping from your kitchen,
Testament of easterly soups.

A MILLION
Strolls we made to the stream:
Fermented cassava and breadfruit—
Our lot and craft,
Graced your firm palms,
Washed clothes left to dry on Idoto greens.

THOSE LOFTY
Hands that squeezed oranges...
Juices flowing into my tender palms,
Those lumped balls

Of fufu into my lusty mouth;
Relished taste after taste
Of the oft testified bitter leaf soup.

YOUR BEAUTIFUL
Cursive writings
Underlined your years of British exposure;
That blank note you gave me to scribble,
I'll ink it with love
Filled with fondest memories—
Wide as West Oakland to West Africa:
Confluence
Of creativity and new friendships.

AS A
Greying hair speaks of age and grace,
Gogo, yours serenaded strength and stay
Until that dark-dressed death
Broke and sucked away your breath!
But not your towering legacies,
Long built with pride and aces!

AMEN!

VI. Makeda and Josephmark

Isinaego

by Isinaego Josephmark Chibueze

Fumbling
Stumbling
Through the thick of the abyss
Oblivion and discontent
Gnaw at my folly.
Swaggering
Prancing
Fighting hurt
A menacing vendetta.

Blinded
Mystified
Fear boiling guts
Burning within
Like wildfire.

I seek
I yearn
I turn to nowhere
To somewhere
To everywhere
For solace,
For contentment
Alas! None... I realize!

Choking
I gag!
Struggling, to breathe
Through all of this struggle
All of this strife.

I stagger

I sway
Breathless, I lay
Devoid, resolute.
Life slowly fizzles out my efforts.
Weak, I lie.

Lo!
I dream
I gleam
Hoping to escape.

Claws of the past.
Craving a new beginning.
Hoping to win through struggles.
Once more.
"Free at last."
I hope, I scream
With fresh breath.

Free at last... I hope to be!

Thunder

by Makeda aka Sandra Hooper Mayfield

No
it happened in
the garden first
Thunder
in the silence
between blinding light
and the roar of Thunder
she held her breath
and died
a little
under the influence of an incestuous hand
the filth of betrayal
the scourging
of innocence
the lash of shame
lights flashed
breath stilled
a deep rumble
she died
a little
again

BlackBoyExploration - *Iman Gibson*

VII. *Juliet & Iman*

Places

by Juliet Nnaji

I am from a place
Where women are told to end their dreams in the kitchen
Like broken plates
That can never be fixed

Mama would sit me outside her makeshift store
Dangling pain on her neck like a label
Wearing a blouse and wrapper with sacrifice boring holes in them.
She would then tell me stories of her youth;
How she sold Icheku seeds to send herself to school
Because her father wouldn't
Then sacrificed her straight-A results to get married to papa,
Because she had passed the age of "Whose daughter is she?"
And was now at the age of "Whose wife is she?"

I come from a place
Where women shrink
Beautiful thoughts
And daring dreams
Because they have been made
To believe that their body
Was an accident.

In our little home of eight, problems crept in and out.
Mama would work all-day, shutter away at night;
Yet, there would be no one to offer her emotional support
Because sharing feelings isn't cost-effective.
All Papa could boast of, was a contorted face with disgruntled frowns
As he raised his iron fists on mama.
Each punch, leaving a dismantled puzzle of teeth and flesh
And a rough sketch of colours on her eyes.

I am from a place
Where polite smiles
Are plaited on faces
Of girls whose temple have
Become a place for broken men

Somewhere,
A woman is afraid for her life.
Like an unarmed soldier in a wild open field
In a war, she never asked for.
She is negotiating her body
When No is not enough

She is watching as shadow
Turns friends into predators
And resistance, merely a suggestion
Yet, she must keep on the facade of
"I am fine"
Not a denial
But self-therapy, for self-immolation,
To avoid being blamed and scorned
And abused some more

Every night, I woke up to the creaking of our wooden door
To see papa tiptoeing into my sister's room.
Now, she has a replica of him sprouting inside her.
No one must know!
Because we wouldn't want to disgrace the family.

In this place, where I come from
We have learned to become
Our watchmen and to fight

Refusing to settle into generational norms
Refusing to shield our eyes
From those hovering like flies
Around our basket
With their patriarchal and misogynistic beliefs

On the day sister gave birth to her daughter,
And we were made to filter our laughter to weigh its worth;
Papa died in his sleep.
After sister and I caught him staring at the newborn
Like her body was not her own.

We were covering all our blind spots,
And taking back the night.
For we no longer wore fear like a second skin.

Like Peeled Grapes

by Iman Gibson

For we no longer wear fear like a second skin
Like peeled grapes...
Lightly chilled
Arranged in decorative glass
Indicative of our class
And whether we'd donned white for cotillions
Waiting...

Pristine and perfect
All...
Pressed hair and
Blue greased edges
Starched dresses and...
The comforting scent of baby powder
Contained.

Good black people.
You know...
The obedient kind
The
Trustworthy and benign...
Empty-eyed and
Order-following
Quick to stomach discomfort as to avoid inducing it.

Like
Perfectly
Peeled grapes
Fresh out of the icebox.
On a hot summer's day.
Just waiting to become amorphous...

Amorphous

by *Juliet Nnaji*

Just waiting to become amorphous
Heart aching
Head spinning
My thoughts played a game of hiding
And seeking answers to the tales of ancestors
Retold by descendants

One on Modernity
"Your skirt is too short"
Men are monsters
They lack self-control
They are moved by what they see
So, "Cover your body properly well, well"
"If your eyes cause you to sin,
Cut them off" became lost in his-story

One on "Who Owns Whose Body?"
Unsolicited affirmations
Eyes sharp, scanning the streets
Doing the mathematics of how many hurried steps
You would need to arrive at your location intact
Because they will ask you
If your body said "Yes"
Even when your mouth said "No"

One on Traditions
"Ugo nwanyi di na be di ya"
What if "marriage holds no attraction for me?"

And I don't want my body
To become a soothing place for any head?
"Oge ana ha ache nwanyi"
What if "Being a mother holds no attraction for me,

Even when I am a great aunt?"
Should that make me less human?

I am from an ancestor
I know
This striking resemblance
Proves their blood flows through me
But their traditions and "norms"
Are sucking out my life like bloodthirsty leeches

So, day and night
Pursuing the passions
That burn in me like a raging tempest
I search for "Who I am"

Who says I can't tear my branch down
And plant my own tree...

Plant My Own Tree

by Iman Gibson

And plant my own tree...
Traverse
Forest.
Desert.
Savannah.

Sweat in jungle.
Freeze on mountain.
Fall in stream.
Wade in water.

That I might seek respite long enough to
Plant hind legs under backside
Slide into inner turmoil
Until it settles into peace.

I plant my own tree
Long
And deep
With the passion always craved from those I let do so inside me.

Of those that sought themselves to find me.
Until roots grow and mycelium flows
And she plugs back in
To home.

VIII. *Koku & ayodele*

Love Without Jealousy

by Koku Konu

What is love without jealousy?
Mmmm...
An empty apparition closely quartered as like
Tepid most times, lukewarm at most
A constant elemental state of
No change
No molten emotion
No liquid delights
No gassy exhilaration
Certainly no alchemy
Just a chemistry
Elemental and confined to its periodic table position

What is love without jealousy?
A rare chime of mild confrontation
Truckloads of indulgent consideration
Sprigs of peace-making olive branches
Liberally doused with the olive oil of compromise
Tossed in a salad of understanding
Two sides of the same coin alone in a pocket
No jangles, no friction
Is this what love without jealousy is?
Hang on, wait a minute!

Perhaps, just perhaps
It is a melodic relationship of utter bliss
Where a kiss is just that: a kiss
Devoid of any follow through
Where compassion overrides passion
Understanding is deep and fulfillment is true.

outside the lines

by ayodele nzinga

"understanding is deep and fulfillment is true"
he said in passing
standing under knowing
of things overstood is deep
but she dont color in no
lines & longs for things
even in dreams her hands
move along the sides of
truth finding herself at the edge
highways without lines
wondering what is
what to do about the things
said & written that shape
texture reality not related
to lives lived dreams dreamed
things taken things given
no denying cant be forgotten
things that float hover
hungry must be fed tended
involuntary reflexive persistent
lost things gathering
in long shadows of new things
written on a song already playing
been playing replaying chords
things float up in the waves
red geranium seeds
prayers sewn inside promises
exploding in dreams

disconnected from the dreamers
at intersections
of the then & this now
the future must stand on
past actions deeds how
else would it find the way
if the unborn could
not speak with the dead
would we ever remember
after
transgression transmutation translated
creation in chaos
ripples cross oceans
rice indigo people red cloth
tales carried through
centuries fill graveyards cells & coffers
altering or fulfilling
destiny
dividing pantheons
forking
paths origin stories colored
overwritten kidnapped hijacked
by hubris driven systems
lynched on survival
into the here the there
the nowhere
asleep she gives it to
the water she hears the bones talk
about oceans crossed
shores of continents
recede approach
different stars
exodus dispersion death rebirth
red geraniums rice
sugar coffee red cloth tales
black bodies
here there nowhere
waking every day in a sorrow older
than the pain carried in bags
packed roughly leaving things behind

torn overstanding
now standing under
rules written imposed created
under constellations
with unfamiliar meanings
hard to embrace the thing
that erases as it consumes
sweat language land
ways of life
songs of days
memory custom purpose
honor dignity
separated
asunder
scattered waiting not melting
remembering
lately she been finding stray pieces
scattered randomly between
now then here
there
reaching for things that the unborn know
running errands for the dead
collecting legions of dismembered
fractals
weaving the
story of
from there to here
then & now

simple sanity could not rest
well here even if it served

this is her overstanding
she dont color in no lines

Colours and Lines

by Koku Konu

She don't colour in no lines
Because she can't

Colour, she is familiar with
Even though new realizations cause her eyes to ratchet focus
With precision greater than a top-notch Zeiss lens
Lines, abstract as the sounds she feels are meaningless
In her defenseless inquisitive dependent world

Lines make connections
Seen and unseen
Allowing us to
Draw conclusions
Follow a path
Retrace steps
Establish a lineage
Identify our heritage

A straight line is the shortest connection between two points
If... you know where you are going
In the absence of a destination
For which there is zero preparation
Her lines turn twist, bend and French Curve
The only intent, the journey

O! The colours?
Forget them not
Divergent in tone and hue
Pepper her voyage of not knowing what to do
Truth be told, what do you expect?
At 5 months old!

likely majick

by ayodele nzinga

! at 5 months old
i was most likely already
majick probably had been that way
from the start
or before
born with a caul over my
eyez & all
likely was majick right away
trials & tribulations
follow majick
& they done
followed me
all my life
always had to be majick
just to hold the idea of me
surviving odds & failing to be a statistic
had to be majick to conjure
survival
majick kept the candle lit
in a storm of a life
a sink
or swim kind of journey
requiring all three
eyes

looking for the signs
searching for the keys
waiting in the gray
everydayness of things endured
like poverty young parents
no inheritance & leaky bags of secrets
that weigh a lot but don't
pay no bills you got
intentions on paying
good thing i remembered sooner than later
later is rarely better than sooner
but it do get its time
you know
greater later
majick always been tricky
mine no different
almost worked better before
i knew about it
before I learned the cost of
things & how not
to blow up a room
with my random thoughts
or tell the truth to fools
because such things wear hard on
them that brings it on
them selves
hands over they eyes
unaware
bereft of majick
full of privilege
but unlucky
lucky
but not majick
yes
i was probably always majick
no need
to color
in the lines
majick
likes its understandings

deep
& plants itself in
bright pennies
grandmas wish on
grandfathers dream
seeds planted
in an intentional universe
where there are no lines
between anything
most answers are yes
& bright children learn to fly
because there is sky
& majick to be tended

i always been majick
i never eat from
empty plates
bone before bowl
my cups
overflow
good character is my companion
good fortune follows me
abundance sits at my table
my dreams come true
they attract other dreamers
flying in &
out the everything
only sky above us
i was born majick
unlikely
impractical an indulgent
manifestation
prayed for & predicted
tested & true
bold
remembering to remember
& i was most likely always majick

IX. Matthew & Iris

Anomaly

by Matthew Otor

I am society's anomaly
Refusing to be waded by these tidal waves of pretense
Why do I have to hide the chaos within me with a facade of order
Why can't I be beautifully chaotic

If I go by the book, I am a bookworm
If I am innovative and break the law, I am a rebel
I am too nice if I'm kind
And rude and cutthroat if I'm blunt
If I cry, I am weak
And if I don't, I am emotionless

If I speak philosophy, I am a rambling idiot
If I don't, I am an ignorant dimwit
If I talk to God, I am religious
If God talks to me, I am psychotic

Humans are lonely for a reason
For the yardstick that defines their reality are drawn with blurred lines

I am society's anomaly
Refusing to be waded by these tidal waves of pretense
I am beautifully chaotic

Beautifully Chaotic

by Iris M. Crawford

I am beautifully chaotic.
Too many puzzle pieces with uncrafted sides.
Not knowing quite where the pieces land.
Chaotic—as an unfinished Rubik's cube, liking the hustle of NYC on
Black Friday, like the mind of a teenage girl the first time she finds herself
In love, Chaotic like... a Black girl trying to find her place in places that
Want to stand firm in not making space for her.

Chaotic like—how should I wear my hair today when I have 5 minutes
Until a Zoom call and depending on if I wear braids, a headwrap or my
Fro, folks might have different opinions about me.

I am beautifully chaotic. Wanting the people closest to me to love me
More but not telling them that I want them to do so.

Some days chaotic looks like autopilot, it can look deranged, helter skelter
Every which way.

But what's a little Black girl from Brooklyn supposed to look like?
No one ever told her better.

I am bold, quietly loud, sheepishly adamant, delightfully but foolishly
Optimistic and beautifully chaotic.

Stitches

by Matthew Otor

My mother was a master with broken things
She was a goddess with a needle
Who knew a stitch could do so much
Not only did she tend my wounds and stitch my clothing
She sewed her words into the very fabric of my personality
And I
Wear it with pride
This same pride I feel whenever I call her mother

Son "the pain is necessary for healing to happen"
Every scar reminds me of her
She turned tragedy into fantasy
And after every hurt
She stitches me back together
One word at a time
And I stand here curious
How do you bring others heaven
When you go through hell yourself
My mother was a master with broken things

                                    She is the reason I'm whole

Dreams

by Iris M. Crawford

If we follow our dreams,
I wouldn't be the president or Rihanna.
Would I trade places with Rupi Kaur?—Probably not.
But like her, I'd like to create new worlds with my words.

If we follow our dreams I'd be lying pathways to true liberation,
self care, joy and love.

Dreams that would let me go back in time and tell my younger self to keep
forging on.
On time,
It will be my time,
This is my time,
I have time.
I have enough.
I am enough.
Enough.

If we follow our dreams, Earth would no longer be my home.
This body would no longer be a capsule to my limits.
My spirit would transcend borders, atmospheres and create Black Futures.
Futures.
Futures so Black, so surreal that we would never comprehend oppression.
If we follow our dreams, would I be free?

X. Michael & Meg

The Lies I Swallowed

by Meg Pierce

I remember the blazing sun
pounding down on a concrete courtyard,
the suffocating heat of the box, El Cajon,
sizzling in waves off the sidewalk
knowing that even though I'd seen a glimpse
of a wide world worth exploring,
I was trapped here
in this family, in this town,
in this body, in this fear.

I remember the cool blue pool
carved out in the concrete,
wearing a bikini I hadn't wanted
wrapping my arms around my flesh,
trying to cover my exposed belly,
trying to hold on hard to an innocence,
a childhood slipping away.

I remember perfecting the drop and dive
so that my towel hit the lounge chair
at the same moment I broke the surface,
plunging into the serene sapphire silence
letting it wash away my skin,
my body, my budding womanhood.
Underwater in the calm,
all that was left
was a heartbeat,
a breath
and a me
I could see clearly.

I remember being born into a boys' world:
three older brothers
meant surviving required
beating boys bigger than me.
A household where
love was reinforced
as insults flung
across the kitchen table
like paintballs.
How my brothers learned
the quickest way to gut a girl
was to disembowel her with the word "fat"
to roast her over a fire
of distorted expectations.
I remember my exasperated mother
trying to cajole me into a puffy pink dress,
my punishment—missing the party.
I remember the loneliness
of the closed bedroom door,
feeling justified that no amount of cake
was worth being a girl for.

I remember discovering
at age 8 or 10,
a three-sport athlete,
and already addicted to the runner's high
of my feet pounding the dust around the track,
discovering that in fact
I weighed less
than most of my friends.
A revelation now—
I'd already swallowed those two lies—
the first that I should
carry the shame of being fat,
the second that
a scale's number determined
my human value.

I have spent my adulthood forgetting
the details of the day the man,
the one who bought 14-year-old me
the bikini
I loathed as much as
5-year-old me
loathed that pink party dress,
warned me—
"You're perfect for now.
Just don't gain a single pound."
The setting is fuzzy from time,
only the suffocating panic
of walls closing in
as he tried to force intimacy
and I projected my being
into a safe turquoise void
where my skin,
my body,
my budding womanhood
disappeared.
Only the message remains
in crystal clear staccato—
"Your. Weight. Is. Your. Worth."
No longer a tantruming 5-year-old
I rebelled by numbing my emotions
in bottomless tubs of ice cream
and swathing myself in yards of fabric—
I passed a decade attempting
to cloak my SELF
from the double-edged expectations—
having learned a woman
is either a sex object
or she is nothing,
I chose to be nothing.

I remember a sea of blonde ponytails
and tight black capris
worn like a uniform
on my college campus
lined with palm trees
and carpeted in lush green
winter and summer grass
overlooking a sparkling blue bay.
Learning about shaving toe hairs
and pledging sororities.
But most of all,
I remember the sophomore upstairs
who went home for winter break
and came back
with a brand new face.

I remember knowing how
to step into womanhood
when I was finally ready
to lay claim to my body at 23.
The diet pills rattling around
in my bookbag.
The only way to stop the twitching
to lace up my sneakers
and let myself loose
on the perfectly paved path
along the sparkling sapphire shore.
I ran to put my past behind me,
to begin the process of forgetting,
to lose and to find,
to figure out.

I remember the lightness I felt
waking up next to you,
the sunny brightness of the room
as we sipped our cups of coffee,
the dizzy joy I felt
after an almost sleepless night
of noisy climax
blending into a sunrise

we welcomed with
moans of pleasure.
The way you set me up
like an employee in your HR office—
"You're beautiful," you said,
"And obviously, the sex
is amazing..."
I would have blushed,
if not for the "but"
already hanging in your voice.
"BUT... I'm just not that attracted to—"
you took a deep breath here
"—your body."
You were "too polite" to put
your thoughts into words
but I heard my stepfather's
warning across 25 years of time.
"Your. Weight. Is. Your. Worth."
I would like to say
I walked away then
and never turned back.

Because the 4-year-old inside me
keeps refusing to wear that dreadful dress.
And the soccer player with skinned knees
keeps stepping on that scale.
The teenager
keeps hiding herself with her arms.
The survivor
keeps scooping ice cream to freeze her feelings.
The young woman
keeps popping diet pills.
All of me keeps asking...
Do I mold myself to the world as it is?
Or do I keep fighting for
the way the world
should be?

The mother of two replies
with her running shoes—
logs a marathon of miles
to remind herself
what her body is capable of,
and when she is done,
she stretches out under the blazing sun
in a bikini of her own choosing
and flaunts her flesh
unapologetically.

And a War Broke Out

by Michael Ayomide

"Do I keep fighting for a world that should be?" I asked as my memory pulled me into its coarse embrace.

Back when I was cramped with ideals and an eye that absorbed too much, I believed gardens were best cultivated in graveyards. That the best way to teach beauty was to lay it beside disgust.

A war broke out within me when I learned that death is a trait of being alive and that I will be deleted before making any sense of the world I have been dumped in. Reality consumed my ideals.

During the war, my voice competed against the chaotic insanity of my existence. I watched in horror all the evil I should soon be capable of.

As the battle drew close to an end, my ideals tore their way out of my vertebrae. They cracked my cranium, popping my brain in their forceful exit.

The war was over and I had lost.

Ever since then, I have been alive but long dead.

Sometimes, what doesn't kill you keeps you alive to kill you later.

What Doesn't Kill You

by Meg Pierce

Sometimes, what doesn't kill you keeps you alive to kill you later.
But nothing destroys you without your permission.

I spent years treading water in a storm,
Keeping my head up just long enough to gulp air
Before the next crashing wave beat me down.
Years clinging to the shipwrecked debris of my ideals.

Smashed against rocks of patriarchy,
Jagged crags I didn't know could pierce my privilege.
Eurocentrism and tradition—distinct formations in the daylight
Equally destructive out of sight below the surface.

Sometimes what doesn't kill you sits in the shadows,
Waiting until wounds have healed over,
Forgotten if not for the scars.
Sometimes they know your weaknesses better than you do.

I'd warned others about them, but in my hubris
I thought I was too strong to be broken.
When others struggled, I stood by to help.
When the struggle became my own, I could only survive.

All those years of letting the current carry me.
Never stopping to reinforce my foundations,
To question the direction of my rudder,
Recalibrate my compass.

I didn't realize, it was my own arrogance,
My own inability to recognize the shiprot
That spilled me into a sea of insecurity,
That left me lost and floundering.

In my ignorance, I treaded water,
Blaming the sirens, blaming the rocks, blaming the gods,
Keeping my head up, but just barely.
Until at last, I surrendered to the deep.

Sometimes what doesn't kill you keeps you alive.
I found myself dragged onto home shores.
Safe, serene, solid sand beneath my feet.
I wrapped myself in family, a warm blanket in cold winter.

Oh how good that ground felt!
Not like the dangerous sea, not like the world out there
With its monstrous teeth always threatening to chew me up.
Oh how good that earth felt!

I'd build a home, instead of a ship.
Let others do the sailing. Let others do the fighting.
Let others get lost in the sweet elixir of living.
Let someone else be brave. Let someone else be the hero.

Sometimes what doesn't kill you keeps you alive.
Have you ever seen the sun rise or set over the sea?
The way the "hello" or "goodbye" is more magical there?
The way the ever-changing waves beckon you toward the horizon?

Maybe the siren serenade is all a charade.
Maybe even while they drew me to destruction, they wished for me to thrive.
Maybe they too want freedom from the patriarchal powers.
Maybe they carried me to shore—kept me alive—for what?

Out there, people knew my name. I was a nemesis and a hero.
Out there, beyond my comfort zone, I wasn't winning every war,
But at least I was living with a purpose beyond myself, out there.
Out there, I never stopped being afraid, but I dared to be brave.

Sometimes what doesn't kill you keeps you alive,
Until you are ready to stop dying and begin living again.

Why the Sky is Blue

by Michael Ayomide

Our eyes instruct the sun on what color we want to see.

The sun couldn't care less. Her fury cannot be dulled by our meager fantasies.
The sky understands and attempts to actualize our dreams, exuding a color of serenity and safety. Indirectly accusing the sun of being the overtly aggressive relative and claiming she (the sky) is protecting us from her.

This wild contrast leads us to say the sky likes us and the sun is cruel.
It matters less that we need the sun more than the sky.

We want to see some things, and the smart ones amongst us are the ones who help us see them.

But isn't that the way of the world.

XI. Rhema Sunshine & Shawna

Dear Grandma

by *Shawna McCoy Sherman*

Grandma, when I look at pictures of you at my wedding
the one with you me and mom white skin
brown skin white skin i'm trying to look past our

differences like how I didn't continue the
nursing tradition at St. Marys, you 1938, mom 1965
didn't have a graduation picture in white nursing cap

in the fifties you the only woman worker on the block
your husband protested, you nursed and you cleaned
you prepared meals you signed over your paycheck

you didn't complain about your weekly $20 allowance
you stored it in an envelope next to the rosary in your top drawer
but i wonder did you ponder this as you daily reflected

over beads on the mysteries glorious and sorrowful
I knew you during your Florida retirement when you took
solace on the gulf walked the beach swam built animals from shells

i remember we displayed one of your lions on the kitchen sill
its leg off, the glue often unstuck in Hawaiian humidity
you visited every other year and then at 19 i visited you

saw your suitcases of thousands of shells, of projects
in progress and learned only recently you worried
what the neighbors would think of us, the Black kids

i'm glad I didn't know it then, I admired your work ethic
took your comments about my curls smiling but now
i wonder, can I claim an ancestor who found it hard to claim me

i find another picture of you and me
at my wedding you and grandpa nearing 100
my back to the camera and you pat my hair

I remember your baffled look when I was 12 and you and mom
attempted to relax my hair in the kitchen on Hui Iwa street
how awkward you must have felt, you who had apprenticed in white

nursing cap, white dress, white apron, white stockings and shoes
i never saw myself in that uniform
but does that matter when there are other nice memories

of eating candy at the beach, laughing at candid camera
and of my wedding when you couldn't remember minute
to minute but told me i was easy to be with and had cute curly hair

Dearest Mother

by Rhema Sunshine

Dearest mother
From the picture I behold
Painted by the passion of your manifold
That has bestowed upon me
Now I understand the beauty of motherhood
So I hail motherhood

You're a perfect definition of perfection
A mother filled with glorious innovation that has caused so many
transformations

God took the fragrance of a flower
The majesty of a palm tree
The gentleness of the morning dew
The calmness of the sea
The beauty of the sun
The joy of the river
The grace of an eagle

Then God fashioned from these things
A creation like no other,
And when his masterpiece was through
He called simply,

"Mother"

A mother whose divinity has impacted humanity
For you are the very definition of humility
A leader whose leadership has infused diligence and produced excellence

You are a mother with a flaming fire
Whose desire has made me a burning and shining light.

Remember we made vows that clouded the sky
We made oceans of joy from the commitment
Of our hearts

Our veins were completely humble,
Gentle and patient bearing with one another in love

And ever since then
You've watched my back
Your personality has contributed to my inner person

Even as I write, words are not enough to express the expression of my heart

So I'll just continue to lie down in green pastures
Keep gazing at memories that will always lead the way...

XII. Poet E. Spoken & Uchechi

What a Blessing

by Poet E. Spoken

History is a very important tool
Especially if you know how to use it
History is not just about where you come from
History is not just about where you've been
History is not just about your place of birth
But history has everything to do with your self-worth
Don't ever expect to find it in any history book
Because we as women have been overlooked
You know a lot of things that I talk about
Reflect from my childhood bad and good
Because there is a lot of things that I do in my life
That I know is not right but just like you
Everyday for me is a continuous fight
But *What a Blessing* it is
To know who I am
You see some people go their whole lifetime
And never understand
Thoughts of anger, frustration, and confusion
Because on the outside we wear it well
But the problem is on the inside
Where we truly dwell
Time after time a friend of mine
Said her mother is her idol
Well I don't believe in idols
But if I did my mother would be mine too
I do believe that the Lord
Has put inspirational people in my life
To kind of guide me and to see me through
And I came to tell you about a few
See she was head of the household
And grandma lived to be 90 years old
She left behind a legacy

Grandma Juanita passed it on to my mother
So that all that I am
All that I will become
And all that I will be
My mother passed that on to me
So I practice what I preach
Now listen y'all
Because I came to teach
Yes, I'm angry over things that have happened to me
Yes I'm frustrated
Because time after time
I turn those pages in my book to take a look
And yet somethings are still outdated
Yes I'm confused
Because sometimes I do the right things
And I still lose but I learned
It's all according to what you choose
So to the successful lawyers oh yes you made it
To the successful doctors oh yes you made it
To those single mothers oh yes you made it
You reached the age 21 oh yes you made it
Anyone with a job or home yes you made it
But turn those pages in your book and take a look
Because you are going to find some things
Listen because the only thing I'm saying to you is
Don't leave it to someone else
To define you
Find yourself and oh *what a Blessing*
It is to know
Listen I don't do this for a show
Because my very existence
Comes straight from experience
And *what a Blessing* it is to know in all of my mistakes
That the Lord still uses me to create
What's up women of the World
Do you know who you are?
What a Blessing

Bloom

by Uchechi Obasi

What a blessing
To have had you come before me
Half-Amazon, half-child
Battlefields and playgrounds
Calling blood grape wine,
Decorating my eyes with lies
Filling my mouth with sour patch

And what a time to have been you
Sprinkling carefree laughter
Like a bride's confetti
Reading the paper to father
Reviving your esteem with
Heavy breaths of courage
Stolen from the pages of old books

Oh, what a blessing
To have been mothered by you
Flat chested, ostrich-necked lass
Cradling secrets with oblivion
Gliding through tomorrow
Waiting with worry for when
Recollection becomes a photograph
And reality distances from the truth

What a blessing!
To be twisted with gratitude
Like the braid on my soft scalp
To live as you, for you, through you
To honor your sacrifice
Bloom wildly like rare orchids
To evolve,
Full Amazon, full woman.

American Painted Lady

by Uchechi Obasi

Mid-March was pregnant with heat
So I wore white.
Do you think it made me stand out
In that dull cafeteria?
Decorated with faulty furniture and
Walls that had become a color wheel
Students splattered like blood in a crime scene
Teasing their taste buds with the fragrance of
Bread, butter and eggs fusing with heat.

Then there was you.
You, skin like earth with legs overflowing
Interrupting the bleakness I had sat with
Saying your name for the first time.
Unfurling the words like a Cadbury crème egg
Smiling as though you had won a lottery.
Me, neck drawing circles in confusion
Oblivious to the effect I was having on you
"D101" I said and you found me again
Just as darkness began to mark its territory.

Life was pink, so was our love
Flourishing like the ixora flowers
Underneath that aged tree by my hostel,
The one where you waited for me
Every evening, perfumed in desire.
We carved our names in a crooked heart
The brown wood bled for us.
Perhaps, it became anemic.

Saturday morning,
My name booming from big overhead speakers
My roommate swelling with amusement
Her faith in love anchored on mine
I scrambled down, my legs now a skater.
You wore a pair of floral shorts
With Spongebob sprawled across your chest
You bumped into me and called it a hug
Cold like an early harmattan morning
Brief like a properly bitten fingernail.

I remember,
It was sunny when you told me—
Yesterday's love had expired
Your belly burned from the staleness of it
Was it akin to eating bread with growing molds?
I sat there by the stairs at the exit door
My eyes appealing your decision,
Bloated from shame braided with rejection.
As I walked out of that cafeteria
It rained and I cuddled my sadness tight.
I remember the cotton tracing my skin,
Walking to my room thinking,
Even heaven is heavy with hurt.

The hardships I endured,
Friends having to choose,
Fish or chicken?
The metallic taste of betrayal
Poisoning my sense of self
Your worthless words writing
Itself on my walls.
Her, in my vision 24/7
You, eluding me like happiness...
Our love was a butterfly,
Rainbow-winged, belly full of nectar
And a terrifyingly short life span.

Funny Money

by Poet E. Spoken

1975 was a good year for me
See I officially started the 1st grade
I was on my way to an illustrious career
As a lifetime student and full woman
Aunt Elaine said, "Come on pig tails
We are going for a treat"
I felt special because usually
My treats were shared with my sister and cousin
And naturally they suckered me into less
Because I was the youngest
I had no conscious of selfishness
So I said come on y'all
But Aunt Elaine said no
"Pigtails it's you and me"
The 20 questions followed
Am I in trouble?
Did I do something wrong?
Cause it was easy to blame me for everything
But she said "No baby girl
I want you to know what it feels like
To be celebrated
I want you to know what it's like
To sit in a restaurant and have people serve you"
We were headed to Downtown Brooklyn
Hell the only time I saw downtown was going
To Con Edison standing in those long lines
With grandma to make arrangements
To keep the lights on

Or passing through on the bus with momma
Everybody thought we were rich
We lived in the biggest house on the block
Annie kept the lawns tailored with her hands
Momma made all our fancy clothes
You did what you had to do
As a single mother raising 5 kids
It took a while for me to understand
Why I was being made to go into the store
With this booklet to buy food
While my siblings stood watch
To make sure our friends didn't see us
Or stand in line on the 30th of every month
To get that government cheese that never melted
It was common place
So when it came down to Aunt Elaine and I leaving
Junior's Restaurant and the waitress presented the bill
I politely asked
"Do y'all take Food Stamps…"

XIII. Victory

Mama Told Me

by *Victory Osarumwense*

Mama told me
Not to wear my love for you on my chest
That I should bury it between my thighs
Tucked between layers upon layers of
Fabric, belt, jeans, panties before skin...

Something hidden
That would call you to dig up
That should make you thirsty
To find my love for you buried beneath the surface of myself.

They call me obstinate
Cause I wore it shamelessly on my neck as a scarf,
Easy to reach for and pull away.

Easy to spot from a distance
Something you'd lay hold of without sweat.

They call me lazy
For I couldn't find the strength to dig between the layers of myself to
hide it.

You call my name
A miracle of a smile appears on my forehead.

Then I remember,
Pray beneath my breath that you don't see—
That my eyes want to explore the depths of your soul.

You ask me a question
Then I remember again,
I should bury it far away for you to dig up.

So I give you a cold stare,
Mumble words that do not really answer your question and walk away.

I walk away in hope,
That you will follow and find the love held in my palm,
I wanted to bury it.

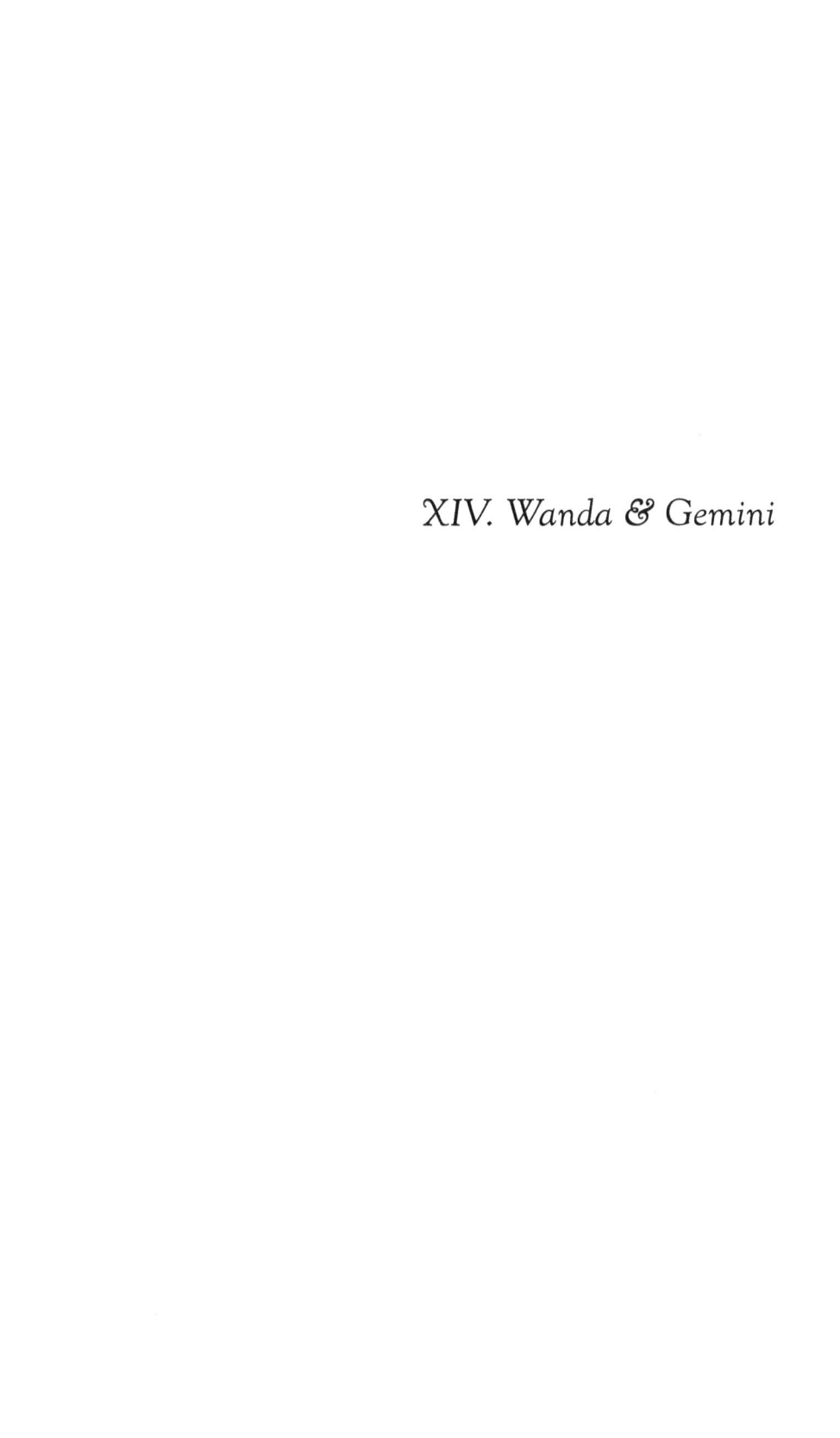

XIV. *Wanda & Gemini*

Homecalling

by Gemini

For all is illusion,
what then do we hold onto?
For all is fleeting,
what then do we clench our fists upon?

My ancestors,
dauntless clan of warlords,
my ancestors,
fearsome can shamans,
my ancestors,
vast compendium of verses,
my ancestors,
nova large body of water
taking the semblance of Oya and Mother Earth,
my ancestors,
now a fiery furnace of raging coals
in guise of Sango and cohorts,
my ancestors,
overflowing purity a calm spilt as Osun in all her radiant glory,
my ancestors,

now a heap of sand
to lay firm the breast bones of their offspring's huts.

No one learns the art of swimming in drylands;
this city is desert landlocked drought
but I'm my mother, incarnate;

blue waters in yet another skin—
I do not drown or sink.

Like fire raging through my father's chest,
I would rather float.
Smithereens don't burn:
my body is a collection of ancient scrolls
my voice—a babel of songbirds whose potions are laced in honey jars
my soul—a playback of moments before
my verses are loop tapes
my ancestors uttered these words, first.

They thought they buried my ancestors,
how mild can ignorance be?
My ancestors were never buried,
they only transited to another city
with Mother Earth's chest, as a pathway.

For all is illusion,
what then do we hold onto?
For all is fleeting,
what then do we clench our fists upon?

For this world is merely a stranger's land,
who then shall escort me back home?
Who then, who then,
when I whisper solemnly,
who then shall lead me
to my ancestors?

For home,
home is the soothing pat of my forebears,
home is
the proverbial smile of my ancestors,
home is
my ancestors gleefully embracing me,
in a feast of eternal welcome.

(My Ogou or) Helium Options . . .

by *Wanda Sabir*

He is the final push into the light
(The) head followed by shoulders. . . slender hips

He energy. . . heated oxygen diamonds and glass
He memory. . . blood memory (buried) hidden in secret places for
Ceremonial
Excavation
He knife. He big bang. He cosmic coming
He utilitarian
He loyal
He fearless
He dangerous
He the one you want on you side
He valiant
He a good soldier

Fire eating he melts in my gaze
Heart races. He win.

(Copper) key chain he wear me close
(Penny) Lockets
Loops dangling I tie my sleeves 'round his waist

Walking. . . (my arms (hands) swing)

My Ogou sends power(ful) energy through connective circuitry
Power fills bellows (which) announce his arrival
(We) expand to accommodate

Black on black majesty

Warrior

God of Iron
We light skillets and prepare for a catch
Hush puppies, okra with green tomatoes, string beans
It is a last supper
We loosen we belts and grab a plate

Lock doors
Ignore bells

We good we say
And feel gastric contentment in new places
Geographically unexplored
Unnamed

We planetary
We say
As levitation become a new norm
Walking too slow
Running unthinkable—

We extraordinary
We say
Planets without atmosphere
We circle each other looking for places to touch (down)

We love
We say as we feel giddy and wonderful and happy in each breath
The ins and outs unimportant
We send details to another department

We just know
We know

We say

Impatient. . . at least she is. She say.
She good. She not good. She good. She not good.
She good for how long, she no know.

She remember the dance two weeks ago
It was slow
The words indecipherable
Ogou engraved in she heart

He lifts his glasses
Takes off he gloves
Turns off the pilot
Puts down the torch and open(s) he arms

She sighs
She . . . walks slowly toward the smoldering furnace without cover and is
Consumed

Good. Ogou smiles
She melts
They form a new galaxy. . . black holes stitched together

Oṣun shakes out the cover
Wicker basket held by helium . . . Ogou and [he wife] Ezili (Hagar) sigh

We happy. They look inside each other's hearts and smile.

Libations for the Egungun or Prayers for the Butterflies

by Wanda Sabir

*For Bishop Edwin Hawkins, Rodney King, Monica Pree, the Jazz Professor Bill Bell, Hubert Collins, Queen Mother Sister Makinya, Brother Tahuti, Sister Nida Ali, Sister Samayah Beyah Bailey . . . General Harriett Tubman and Sojourner Truth . . . and for the men and women and children on death row – and to those sentenced to Life without the Possibility of Parole, this **psalm** is for you.*

Colorful angels fill skies, wings dipped in morning dew. Sweetness scents horizons. This poem is for those who left too soon and the wandering Souls trapped unable to return or find home

Kidnapped and sold to soul catchers. . . we have forgotten much along the way, but our tongues remain attached to our hearts and speak truth

Listen

Spirit guides talk to us
Butterflies or ancestors help us recall what is wonderful
And we smile

Blessed

We need a ceremony.
A container where we can hold what was lost now found
Golden stories
Silver melodies
Brass beats and silences

Perhaps these words are libations
for those souls who have lost direction

I dip my tongue in ink

spraying accolades and diamonds
on the lost ones

My palms are maps
Coordinates in a tapestry or landscape
not plugged into local GPS signals

My tongue dipped in red ink writes blackness on white slates
My words are prayers, each syllable an incantation, each punctuation
mark a signpost in the dark for those walking in
Candlelight

My words are prayers, prayers for those
who left here too soon

Prayers for those who sit on concrete slabs lie
on metal benches sit in isolated
corridors at closed doors waiting
Waiting for human touch . . . waiting for
acknowledgement of their humanity

These are my people these are the
people I write for

Screened behind locked doors heavy
doors high walls fingers scratch
clamor. Toes caught between
barbed wire, storm fences, between
rainstorms and rainbows. . .

My tongue dipped in blues sings hymns coded with secret
messages only the initiated understand

My blues break apart purples and greens refracted landscapes where light
breaks the prism and frees the spirit

locked within
My tongue dipped in red sings Oya's fury
sweeping away the debris the
Clutter the
confusion that sometimes keeps the
wandering ones trapped

I sing a song, I sing a song
I sing a song copyright pending this
song lightens the load makes the
listener shake . . . shake off burdens
assigned but not earned

Today, I sit at a stoplight on Castro and 18th Street in Oakland, California
An officer directs traffic, signals out
When he turns, a driver
runs the imagined light. Imagined
collision avoided

We who watch shutter, then sigh

The moment passes
The driver a bad memory or was he just
lucky

Slaves are not lucky.

This song is for guidance
this song uses a landline
this song renders toxicity benign

Curative, this song clarifies the
water it makes butter from the milk it
enriches all who hear it
all who feel it all
who participate in it

This song is a tapestry a human tapestry
with threads connecting 100 million
lives rent asunder

This song is a lullaby for those with
insomnia
it's a passageway through
the *Doors of No Return*
though the door is still closed,
and we have to pay toll to the
troll at the gate

Akwaaba or *welcome* hits our backside
Surprisingly, the passage didn't
kill us but made us a stronger Black
people.

The toll the labor the stench the
horrors we forget
Intentionally, to survive the moment
this moment. . .
An immediacy that is
our recent history held against a greater
history would sustain us,
if we would (could) only remember
but we are not deterred.

The journey has made
us wiser
It didn't weaken us but made
us develop antibodies antibodies
antibodies for an army that cannot be
defeated

We are, as Nikki Giovanni says: *A bad people*
I dip my tongue into elixir. I dip my
tongue into an elixir, a secret potion
passed forward through unclassified DNA.
It is the melanin-colored memories

A secret potion only the innocent dare
drink

This testimony is for those who left
here too soon

This testimony is for those who are in
pain

This testimony is for the yet-to-be-born

This poem is an *Ashay*, a *Hallelujah*, an
Amen a So Be It to those standing at the
crossroads making informed choices

"[If] all is an illusion. . ."[1]
The rightly guided
Those who stride on *aṣ-Ṣirāṭ al-mustaqīm*,[2] Allah's People hold onto the
only Reality and give thanks!

Ashay

---

1   Gemini
2   (Arabic: الصراط المستقيم)

Iwúre Alágbaà

by Gemini

Àṣẹ iná ni iná n fi jo l'oko,
àṣẹ oorun ni oòrùn n fi ran ni sannmọ,
bi ọmọde mú ọsẹ lọwọ,
aa ni ko ṣẹ.
Bi awọn agba kujẹkujẹ mú ọsẹ lọwọ,
wọn àà ni ko ṣẹ.
Ṣíṣe ṣiṣe n t'ilakọṣẹ,
igi k'igi ti elegbede ba f'ọwọ ba ni igbo,
meebi didun ni n dun.

Ọmọde inu yin ko máa pe Yóò ṣẹ,
ko ni ṣai ṣẹ,
Agba inu yin, ko máa pe yóò ṣẹ,
ko ni ṣai ṣẹ,
Ọkùnrin inu yin, ko máa pe yóò ṣẹ,
ko ni ṣai ṣẹ,
Obìnrin inu yin, ko máa pe yóò ṣẹ,
ko ni ṣai ṣẹ.

Iran omi eti'do kìí loju ọgbẹ,
bẹẹ ìran iṣan odo kìí loju apa,
awọn agbara, wọn kìí ni ipa egbò,
emi rẹẹ d'oterere omi loni,
awa o tún gbọdọ l'olodi kan.
Ebute iṣe rere ni odo yii n ṣan lọ,
a ko tun gbọdọ̀ pade ọgbẹ lọnà.
Okun kìí ri, bẹẹ ọsa kìí ri,
alagbalugbu odo ko ni láéláé sìn lọlẹ,
omuwẹ ni ẹ kilọ fún, omuwẹ,
ọta wa ni ẹ ṣe kilọkilọ fun,
eyi to ba ṣe eti kikun àà sì máa bá ẹja odo ṣe ìpàdé bo d'ọla.

Ara mi, mutumuwa,
àní ẹ máa pe yóò ṣẹ,
ko ni ṣai ṣẹ.
Iran afẹfẹ lẹgi lẹgi ko ni láéláé f'ara gb'ọfa,
b'iji ii já n'ile, já l'ọdan,
ìran iji kan o ni láéláé f'ara gb'ọta.
T'ibi t'ire n lọ lọna,
afẹfẹ ni n ṣe ọlọkọ wọn,
iku oun iye n dagbere irin ajo,
atẹgun máa ni atẹgun wọn.
Gbọ,
bi ibi ba n bẹ nile,
ko ni ba wa nile.
Bi ààrùn n bẹ l'oko,
ko ni ba wa l'ebe.
Bi kelukelu ọran ba da joko si oríta,
awa o ni mọ ina bẹẹ.

Yóò máa kú diẹ ni, yóò máa kú diẹ ni,
ọmọ odo o ni láéláé di ohun amurinti,
yóò máa kú diẹ, yóò máa kú diẹ,
igba ile ọba o ni láéláé fọ,
àní yóò máa kú diẹ, yóò máa kú diẹ,
awo ilé ọba ko ni láéláé fa ya.
Ọrẹ, wí fún ẹnìkan pe
yóò máa kú diẹ, yóò máa kú diẹ,
agẹrẹ igbe ko ni láéláé sọ ni ile koowa wa.

Iran iri afẹmọju ko ni láéláé ṣẹ gbígbóná,
kurukuru ìì ba lerooro l'oke jù bẹẹ lọ,
láéláé, ko máa lé bo ìràwọ sannmọ mọlẹ.
Gbọ,
emi rẹ di af'epoj'obi,
aa di af'obij'epo,
awa di aláṣọ ala kẹlẹẹlẹ,
ẹni kan ko tun le dun mọ huruhuru mọ imọlẹ wa.
Fìtílà tí Ọba mi Oke tan ni wa, ẹda eniyan ko le láéláé lu wa pa.

Bi igi gbogbo ba kun igbo ni iṣọri iṣọri,
o di awati —
igi níí tí a o fi gbẹ posi emi rẹẹ,
o di awati n'igbo l'ọdan.

Eyi aa wí di àṣẹ,
Alágbaà ti fọhun,
Abilọjẹ ti fi aṣẹ sí.

Àṣẹ.

About the Contributors...

Dee Allen. is an African-Italian performance poet based in East Oakland, California. Allen has been active in creative writing & Spoken Word since the early 1990s. He has authored seven books so far including: *Boneyard*, *Unwritten Law*, *Stormwater*, *Skeletal Black*, *Elohi Unitsi*, and *Rusty Gallows* and *Plans*.

Adeyinka Ireti Aromolaran is a college teacher of arts and design, and drama. She has a passion for research related to the history of traditional art and culture. She also loves cooking. The connection Aromolaran sees between art, design and poetry is that poetry is like an imaginative painting or drawing. Writers who influenced her include Okot p'Bitek and Niyi Osundare. Okot p'Bitek was a Ugandan poet, who achieved international recognition for "Song of Lawino." Niyi Osundare's poems often deal with social concerns and African people. Her own poems are rich with imagery and metaphors steeped in African cosmology.

Michael Ayomide is an undergraduate student studying medicine in Nigeria. He is from the Yoruba tribe. He believes words, particularly the art of reading or writing poems, have therapeutic effects and, if used correctly, can be a form of medicine in itself. His works have been heavily influenced by Rudy Francisco, Phil Kaye, Taiwo Hassan, vic Wrights, Samuel Adeyemi, Olaitain Humble, Ocean Vuong, Rupi Kaur, Warsan Shire, to mention a few. Michael writes when inspired, but lately, he writes more about the art of dying, survival, and rebirth. His first and only poetry collection is Blue. However, he is working on a new book titled *dead stars don't shine*.

Yusuf Alabi Balogun alias Aremo Gemini is a Yoruba griot and a cultural curator, with a foremost dream to sell out O² Arena for Yoruba poetry. He has numerous content to his credit which can be found on his social media platform — @aremogemini.

Nana Boateng (she/her) is a first generation Ghanaian-American poet, educator, and digital storyteller currently residing in Oakland, CA. She utilizes writing and audio to examine memory, otherness, and myths we tell ourselves. Her writing has been published in Connotation Press, WVXU, NPR, Sierra Magazine, Toe Good Poetry, and Cliterature Journal.

Elaine Brown aka Poet E. Spoken is an explosive freestyle artist, history teacher, and the Co-host of VENT, an online literary Empathy Circle, and My Word Open Mic. They are "Never afraid to normalize conversations of trauma!"

John Otiso Bundi would have never enjoyed poetry if it weren't for the intervention of his one and only father in writing, Dr. Okemwa. He mentored John into writing and always kept in touch on the key aspects of improving his writing skills. Other significant poets that influenced John include Zakiyyah G. E. Capehart, Maya Angelou for *The Heart of Modern America*, Elizabeth Bishop for *The Traveling Poet*, and the all-time Romantic poet, Edgar Allan Poe. As one of the poets influenced by the romantic writers, John turns to the theme of love often in his writing.

Zakiyyah G.E. Capehart is a writer, published poet, storyteller, performance artist, visual artist, radio producer and host, and author. Her poetry is published in many anthologies and has been shared internationally. Zakiyyah's recent book, *Ghana On My Mind: Poetic Reflections on Journeying to the Motherland* was the #1 Best Seller in African Poetry on Amazon on March 13, 2021.

DaJuan "DonJuan" Carter-Woodard is an Oakland native. He is a Youth Coordinator at Eastside Arts Alliance and has been an activist for 10+ years. His first published book was 2019's Bleeding Between the Bars. He has been featured in a variety of publications and anthologies including Patrice Lumumba—An Anthology of Writers on Black Liberation.

Stanley Kipkorir Chemweno is pursuing an undergraduate degree in English and Literature. He has been featured in numerous anthologies including *Shackles of Pain*, *Diary of Broken Hearts*, *Scars, Stars and Global poetry*, *Arthut*, *Campus Magazine*, *We Write You Read*, and *Mt. Kenya Times*.

Josephmark Chibueze is a credit analyst, sales executive, information broker, freelance writer, and poet. Poetry is religion to him—a sacred act and art. He is heavily influenced by notable writers such as Wole Soyinka, Chinua Achebe, John Pepper Clark, Christopher Okigbo, and Bernard Cornwell. He explores diverse themes, with his personal favourite being themes of nature, identity, desire, and self. An immense lover of the arts, he is.

Iris Crawford is a climate journalist who is currently obtaining her master's in science writing. Her writing covers science, climate justice, arts & culture, and more. Her background is in grassroots community organizing and she finds the most joy in helping frontline communities gain access to the resources they need. She is an Afrofuturist so you can always find her thinking about new Black futures.

Kevin Dublin is a writer of poetry, prose, scripts, and code. Currently Director of Litquake's Elder Writing Project, he's focused on expanding the project to primarily BIPOC-served facilities. Kevin is the author of the chapbook *How to Fall in Love in San Diego* (Finishing Line Press) and holds an MFA from San Diego State. He has received awards from the San Francisco Arts Commission, Yerba Buena Center for the Arts, Martha's Vineyard Institute of Creative Writing, North Carolina Poetry Society, and the Writers Studio. He's also developing creative writing programs for Black youth in San Francisco. Follow him on Twitter @PartEverything.

Tongo Eisen-Martin is an educator and organizer whose work centers on issues of mass incarceration, extrajudicial killings of Black people, and human rights. He was born in San Francisco and earned his MA at Columbia University. He is the author of someone's dead already (Bootstrap Press, 2015), nominated for a California Book Award; and Heaven Is All Goodbyes (City Lights, 2017), which received a 2018 American Book Award and a 2018 California Book Award. He is the current Poet Laureate of San Francisco.

Duana Fullwiley Duana Fullwiley is a literary anthropologist of science and medicine whose fieldwork with scientists, patients, and larger publics explores the interplay of genetics, health and cultural politics in Senegal, France, and the United States. She is the author of *The Encultured Gene: Sickle Cell Health Politics and Biological Difference in West Africa*. She has received awards from the Fulbright Scholars Program to Senegal, the National Science Foundation, the Social Science Research Council and the Wenner-Gren Foundation for Anthropological Research. She teaches at Stanford
University

Iman Gibson is a wellness educator and evangelist from Los Angeles who loves to take portraits of beautiful humans and express emotion through imagery and text. She loves to create multimedia art experiences centered around well-being and mental health.

Lisa Gray believes that it is necessary for black women to write and share our stories so that others do not erase or control our narratives. She won the 2018 Robert L. Fish Edgar Award. You can find her at www.lisawrites.life and on IG @ovossf.

Tessa Hersh likes dogs, birds, and watching clouds move faster than her. She laughs loud and cries often. Biologically Kenyan and Russian Ashkenazi, Hersh was raised by a Minnesotan mom and Brooklyn dad. She likes talking about birth, death, and delicious food. She is an actor, writer, and educator with a Master's in Somatic Psychology.

Makeda aka Sandra Hooper Mayfield, is a poet, journalist, tutor, counselor, and community activist. She is best known for her work with youth. Makeda's work is published in three Alameda County Seniors Poetry anthologies as well as a chapbook collection. She developed the "Third Saturday Open Mic" and an annual artist retreat called Sugar Water.

Caren (Carina) Jepkogei is a Kenyan poet who has participated in different poetry exchanges and competitions, including the Asian Literary Society, Ndimi Za Kalamu, and Kistrech Poetry Festival. She's currently pursuing her Master's in project planning and management at Catholic University of East Africa.

Durotinu Jeremiah is a researcher, content writer, and social media manager. He holds a degree in Philosophy at the University of Lagos.

Cornelius Kipkosgei has contributed his poems to several anthologies: *Shackles Of Pain*, *When I Marry Rimanto*, *Black Lives Matter*, *Echoes From The Plains*, and *Garden Of Wild Roses*. He is the author of *Wanda, My Love*, a collection of poems.

Koku Konu is not an award-winning writer or poet and he does not wish to be. He started writing poetry unintentionally during the 2020 lockdown to express the curious thoughts and images he could not, or would not, draw. Writing adds another layer to his expanding understanding of this journey called life.

Chasejamison (CJ) Akilah Manar-Spears is a multi-dimensional Pan-Afrikan creative born and raised on Ohlone lands. They are inspired by ancestral expressions of love, internal changes within society, and the creative source of nature. They began creating as a form of healing and joined this project to discover collective meaning.

Josephat Ndege Mauti is a playwright and poet. Through his writings, he chronicles the theme of moral decadence in society. He has published two plays: *The Valentine Wedding* (2017) by Pangolin Publishers Ltd (KE) and *The Forbidden Fruit* (2022) by Nsemia Inc. Publishers. His poems have also been published in the Kistrech Poetry Festival (KPF) Official Magazines of 2014 and 2019, and in *Musings During a Time of Pandemic: A World Anthology of Poems on COVID-19* (2020). He currently teaches English and Literature at Machongo P.A.G Secondary School.

Mose Rebeccah Mongina aka Becca the Poet is a Kenyan writer born in the late 1990s. She developed writing at the age of 14 and her writing skills have grown through today. Her work reflects on society. Becca the Poet has influenced many youth with her writings. She is a good stage performer and her performances have been featured at local Kenyan TV channels like KTN, KBC, and KU TV. She has participated in poetry festivals such as Kistrech International Poetry Festival, The Writers Pen Poetry Festival, World of Dreams Poetry Festivals, and many more. She looks forward to transforming rotten society through her work.

Kelvin Kombo Motuka is a specialist in Kiswahili literature. He has translated many literary works from English to Kiswahili including *Sabina and the Mystery of the Ogre* (Sabina na Fumbo la Jitu) by Christopher Okemwa.

Evans Mwendwa Mutie is a Kenyan poet and a short story writer from Kisii University. He is the author of *The Universe in One Page* and has also contributed poems to *Shackles of Pain* and *In The Murk of Life*.

Juliet Nnaji is a notable poet, content developer for Whispa, author of two books, and the anchor for "Poetry In Motion," which is a website for poets to connect. Her poem, "If The Country is a Book" was selected by Professor Wole Soyinka and performed at a World Poetry Day event.

Alfred Nyagaka Nyamwange is pursuing a Ph.D. in Literature at Kisii University. He has published a children's story called *The Smell of New Shoes*, a collection of adult short stories titled *The Woman Called Angel* and two novels titled *The Blood Stains* and *Sunlight on a Broken Column*.

Bonface Nyamweya is a Kenyan poet, playwright, and novelist. *The Nile, Our Neither/Nor* (2019) was his debut poetry collection. He is the author of *Peeling the Cobwebs* and *Her Question Pills*. He is finishing a Master's in Philosophy at the Catholic University of Eastern Africa.

ayodele nzinga M.F.A, Ph.D., is a writer, director, actress, lyricist, and producer living in Oakland, California. She is the author of *SorrowLand Oracle* and *The Horse Eaters*, available at www.nomadicpress.org, as well as *Incandescent* available on Amazon Books. Nzinga is the inaugural Poet Laureate of Oakland, CA.

Uchechi Obasi is a Nigerian poet based in Lagos, the city that never sleeps. Her work has been curated on *Medium* multiple times. When she is not writing, Uchechi spends time working out, listening to audiobooks, and rewatching Modern Love for the umpteenth time. Keep in touch with Uchechi via the web: *Medium:* https://link.medium.com/P6ul5eqUxib or on Instagram @Uchechi_o

Godfrey-Elvis Odianose is the pregnant egg in a barren hen. "Poetry is light to me. Poetry makes me realize that in my dark skin lies the brightness to the future." He has been influenced by amazing writers such as Rudy Francisco, Rupi Kaur, Billy Chapata, and ayodele nzinga. His poem in the anthology, "Before Your Nubian Hues" speaks to police brutality, and the poem has skyrocketed in Nigeria. This made the #EndSARS protest go viral in 2020, which led to the deaths of young people at the Lekki Massacre in October of that year. Odianose is also the co-author of a poetry and prose book titled *Jupiter and Saturn*, available on Amazon.

Dr. Christopher Okemwa is a lecturer of literature at Kisii University and the director of Kistrech International Poetry Festival in Kenya. He has published collections of poetry, novels, oral literature, and children's stories.

IMAHKÜS Njinga aka Mama One Africa and husband Nana Okofo repatriated to Ghana from New York in 1990. A prolific writer with a candid sense of humour, she has authored, *Returning Home Ain't Easy But it Sure Is A Blessing*, in which she shares her personal experiences and demonstrates what it takes to settle and make Ghana one's home.

adrienne danyelle oliver is a poet-educator from Little Rock, Arkansas who is based in the San Francisco Bay Area. Her previous work has appeared in *Storytelling, Self & Society* (Wayne State University Press, 2018), *Patrice Lumumba: An Anthology of Writers on Black Liberation* (Nomadic Press, 2021) and *Essential Truths: The Bay Area in Color* (Pease Press, 2021).

Halima J. Olufemi was born and raised in Jackson, Mississippi. She is a member of the Malcolm X Grassroots Movement, JXN People's Assembly, Holla Back Poetry Circle, and she also works with the People's Advocacy Institute as the Director of the Participatory Defense Program. Her poetry centers around liberation and Black Feminist thought.

Lilian Omonga is a Kenyan poet and an upcoming novelist. She is a student at Kisii University pursuing a Bachelor's of Education, English and Literature. She is also a member of The Great Achievers Group, a small group that performs plays and drama.

Ifeanyichukwu Onwughalu is a husband, father, poet, realtor, and entrepreneur. He draws inspiration from Christopher Okigbo, Nelly Sachs, and other poets. Society, the environment and life experiences contribute powerful tools on his poetic journeys.

Odiase David Osaodion, known as The 78th Psalmist, is a Nigerian poet and spoken word artist born in Surulere, Lagos. Famed for his command of wordplay, metaphors, and sarcasm, his writings are considered non-conformist and conscientious. His work has been described as "A light pen scribbling dark truths."

Victory Osarumwense uses words as a tool to inspire people from all walks of life. Through performing, speaking, writing, and financial literacy, she addresses and brings solutions to real life issues. She is the author of *Keeping Faith*, a hilarious faith-based collection published in 2018, as well as *Breathe*, a spoken word EP released in 2017. Victory held her first storytelling concert themed *Conversations from last night* in 2019 and has also contributed to the African anthology *How to Write My Country's Name*. She writes poems, short stories, articles, and more on her website victoryosas.com and on her instagram handle @victory_osas. Her literary works touch heavily on the subject of identity, faith, gender and social injustice. When she is not writing/performing poetry, she works as a Fixed Income Trader at a top bank in Nigeria and runs a financial literacy segment called @financialjagajaga on Instagram.

Matthew Otor is a postgraduate student in the Architecture Department of the University of Lagos, having completed his Bachelor's degree at the same university. A resident of his birthplace of Lagos, Nigeria, he does not see himself as one tightly bound by the rhetoric of culture and tradition.

Margaret L. Pierce (Meg) is a hard-working dreamer, a clumsy poet, an aspiring novelist, a struggling single mother, a former international teacher, a volunteer soccer coach, a nature-loving wanderer, a straddler of worlds, the middle of nine siblings, a real estate marketing associate, and a seeker of knowledge and wisdom.

Wanda Sabir is a poet, essayist, arts editor, and senior writer at the San Francisco Bay View newspaper. *Wanda's Picks* column & radio show are a local and national staple. Her interest is in art for social change. As a depth psychologist, Ms. Sabir's area of research is on trauma and its impact on memory. Ms. Sabir also serves as board member for Legal Services for Prisoners with Children. An advocate of *Diaspora Citizenship*, Ms. Sabir is also co-founder and CEO of the San Francisco Bay Area Maafa Commemoration. This summer she is "Souljourning for Truth," a *wombful* pilgrimage from California to New York, Massachusetts, and Michigan, inspired by the life and work of Sojourner Truth. Visit wombfulnessgathering.blogspot.com and http://maafasfbayarea. com for more.

Kiani Shaw aka LadiRevolutionary (LadiRev) is a poet from Bayview Hunters Point. Her poetry is a reflection of personal struggle and values learned from friends and family. LadiRev is passionate about community, education, and healing. "It only takes one person to make a stand, but it takes a community to make a change."

Shawna McCoy Sherman is a poet and librarian born and raised in Hawaii who now lives in the San Francisco Bay Area. Her writing focuses on race and place, and also borrows from history in order to make sense of the present.

Darius Simpson is a writer, educator, performer, and skilled living room dancer from Akron, Ohio. He aims to inspire that feeling you get that makes you frown and slightly twist up ya face in approval. Darius believes in the dissolution of empire and the total liberation of Africans and all oppressed people by any means necessary.

Landon Smith is a father, professor, poet, half-Mende and half-Balanta and Fulani, that feeling of falling that wakes you up in a dream, the amethyst geode on your desk, Angela Davis' afro, Frantz Fanon's pocket notebook, Walter Rodney's fingernail, the 7-10 bowling split, and your favorite pillow.

Rhema Sunshine is a member of Poets In Nigeria (PIN) and also an award-winning poet, songwriter, performer, and video producer who lives in Lagos, Nigeria. He is the 2020 winner of the Milwaukee Youth Poetry Prize for Emerging Writers, and the 2021 recipient of a RGDN Literary Award in the category of "Short Works Poetry."

Mimi Tempestt (she/they) is a multidisciplinary artist, writer, and daughter of California. She is currently a doctoral student in the Creative/Critical Ph.D. in Literature at UC Santa Cruz. Her first book, *the monumental misrememberings*, is published with Co-Conspirator Press/The Feminist Center for Creative Work (2020).

Lewis Wamwanda is a student at Kisii University pursuing a Bachelor's of Education, English and Literature. He is the founder of *The Writers Pen*, a self-publishing company and also the author of *Reflections: An Anthology of Poems*.Wamwanda has participated in multiple poetry competitions held by Asian Literary Society.

Amos White is an award-winning American haiku poet and author, producer, civil rights activist, and environmentalist. Recognized for his vivid literary imagery and breathless poetic interpretations, White is published in several national and global anthologies. An impresario, Amos founded and produced Heart of the Muse creative's salon, Beyond Words jazz+poetry show, served as President of Bay Area Generations literary reading series, and was also co-founder of the Black Speculative Arts Movement California.

About the Editor...

Karla Brundage is a Pushcart Prize nominee, Fulbright teacher and author of two books of poetry, *Swallowing Watermelons* and *Mulatta- Not so Tragic* which was co-authored with Allison Francis. She has performed her work onstage and online, both nationally and internationally. Her poetry, short stories and essays can be found in *Konch*, *Hip Mama*, *sPARKLE & bLINK*, *Bamboo Ridge Press*, *Vibe*. A Bay Area based poet, activist, and educator with a passion for social justice. Born in Berkeley, California in the summer of love to a Black mother and white father, Karla spent most of her childhood in Hawaii where she developed a deep love of nature. Her musical loves include Hawaiian, West African, and Hip Hop sounds. Her work can be found at http://westoaklandtowestafrica.com/ as well as on https://www.karlabrundage.com/ .